on my own now

straight Talk from the proverbs for young Christian women who want to Remain pure*, Debt-free and Regret-free

by donna lee schillinger

The **Quilldriver**
WORKS WITH WORDS
Clarksville, Ark.

*made ya look! So, what were you expecting to find down here anyway?!?

On My Own Now: Straight Talk from the Proverbs for Young Christian Women
who Want to Remain Pure, Debt-free and Regret-free
By Donna Lee Schillinger

Cover Design by Daniela Bermudez

A publication of The Quilldriver, Clarksville, Ark., U.S.A.

ISBN 978-0-9791639-5-1

Publisher's Cataloging-In-Publication Data
(Prepared by The Donohue Group, Inc.)

Schillinger, Donna Lee.

   On my own now : straight talk from the Proverbs for young Christian women who
want to remain pure, debt-free and regret-free / by Donna Lee Schillinger.

   p. ; cm.

   Includes bibliographical references.
   ISBN: 978-0-9791639-5-1

1. Christian women--Life skills guides. 2. Christian women--Conduct of life--Biblical
teaching. 3. Bible. O.T. Proverbs--Criticism, interpretation, etc. 4. Life skills--Biblical
teaching. 5. Christian life--Biblical teaching. I. Title.

BV4551.3 .S24 2008
248.833

Printed in the United States of America

gratitudiosity

This book is for Gwendolyn

Thanks to all my she-homies who aided and abetted the preparation of this book, including but not limited to: Debra Collins, Cheryl Valliquette, Amy Gross, Paola Segnini, Daniela Bermudez, Juli Ginn, Kelli Williams and my mom, Nancy Hunter. As always, thanks to my loving husband, John, and the kiddos, Gwen and Chaise, for their indulgence. Thanks to my agent, publisher and publicist – oh wait, I don't have any of those…awkward.

Finally, I'd like to acknowledge (in general) all of the fine examples of Christian love and living I know, and our All-Good, All-the-Time, Holy Three-in-One.

table of contents

5 .... On Your Own Now? Start Here.

11 .... First, Let's Put My Parents in Their Place

25 .... Owner of a Lonely Heart

65 .... Beauty Secrets from the Proverbs

95 .... Living La Vida Buena

123 ....When Morality Meets Reality

168 .... To Befriend and Be a Friend

188 ....The Greatest of These is Charity

201.................. The E³ (Ethereal • Ephemeral • Eternal)
Wisdom of the Proverbs

217 .... Long-Term Forecast: Sunny Skies

248 ....This is Me – Fearless!

268 .... Taking it to the Next Level

introduction

On Your Own Now? Start Here.

What Good Will the Proverbs Do Me?

Ready to Move Off "Start"?   5

What Good Will the Proverbs Do Me?

These are the proverbs of Solomon son of David, king of Israel: for attaining wisdom and discipline; for understanding words of insight; for acquiring a disciplined and prudent life, doing what is right and just and fair; for giving prudence to the simple, knowledge and discretion to the young – let the wise listen and add to their learning, and let the discerning get guidance – for understanding proverbs and parables, the sayings and riddles of the wise.

6

Proverbs 1:1-6

Wisdom is good – duh! So, go ahead and get some. But how?

You probably would agree that to be wise is a good goal, but it might seem so intangible that you don't know where to begin. Maybe you've heard a pastor or priest say, "Read Proverbs to grow in wisdom." Maybe you've tried it. I did. I latched on to some key verses, but to be honest, I didn't really believe that most of Proverbs applied to me and my life. The author, good King Solomon, spends a lot of time telling young men to stay away from prostitutes and I was pretty sure that would never apply to me. And in the literal sense, I was right. It wasn't until I read Proverbs again for the first time in a long while, when I was 40 years old, that I realized all those warnings to stay away from prostitutes had been for me, specifically for me in my youth, even though I've never visited a prostitute and can safely say I never will.

I desperately needed the Proverbs in my young adult years – from the time I left for college through Peace Corps service, and 15 years of "single and loving it!" But I didn't realize it because I didn't have the time or make the effort or whatever was needed to extrapolate the lessons behind all those "stay away from prostitute" warnings.

In retrospect, when I realized how much I could have benefited from some straight talk from the Proverbs, I acquiesced fairly easily when God led me to dig into the Proverbs and bring them to life – your life – a single young, Christian woman who is now on her own.

I'm writing this Proverbs guidebook for you for the same reasons Solomon wrote Proverbs. I want you to be wise.

I want you to:

- Grow up – not just get older but to mature emotionally and spiritually as you increase in age.
- Be able to take care of yourself and your family successfully.
- Have the ability to recognize good advice, receive it and apply it to your life.
- Have a strong internal sense of right and wrong and when you're in one of life's many gray zones, to be able to figure out the right course of action.
- Use your youthful energy for achieving success and enjoying life, rather than making foolish mistakes of youth.
- And I want you to gain an appreciation for that nebulous concept that is "wisdom," so much so that in all you do, even the mistakes you make, you'll look for the wisdom to be gained from it.

Why do I want a wise young adulthood for you? Because I know firsthand what comes of youthful zeal foolishly wasted, and you'll see just what I'm talking about in upcoming chapters. The thought that maybe something in these pages could help you better understand the wisdom of the Proverbs, and perhaps choose to apply them and avoid making some of the stupid mistakes that are usual and customary for young women today is what motivates me to write a guide for you. Do you want to skip a lot of heartache and embarrassment in life? Then read on.

Ready to Move off "Start"?

The fear of the Lord is the beginning of knowledge, but fools despise wisdom and discipline.

Proverbs 1:7

Fear of the Lord? It seems contradictory to fear this wonderful Creator who is all good and all love. What's to be scared of, right? It is sometimes helpful for me to think of the word "fear" more in the sense of "revere." Instead of being afraid of my Heavenly Father in the way I would fear a psycho, I revere God as a great and awesome power – like that of nuclear weapons (times a googolplex).

Fear of the Lord is recognizing God as Creator of the universe and the power in control of everything, including activity in our bodies at a cellular level. It is acknowledging that this same power who is tending to the big issues, like keeping galaxies in order, is also aware at every moment how many hairs are on our heads. And not only is this awesome being aware, He cares. Yes, the Creator of the universe cares to keep track of how many hairs end up in our brushes every morning. Why? Because God made us and God is the ultimate parent. The love of an earthly parent is so profound it is impossible to measure. Harder still is wrapping our minds around the love of our Heavenly Parent.

Just like any good parent, God wants us to be happy. And like any good parent, God knows that giving us what we want all the time will not make us happy. Instead, God gives us what we need and one of our needs is discipline. Consider being disciplined by a force powerful enough to snuff the sun in an instant. There's cause for fear! That the Creator of the universe loves and cares for us and our daily needs, including our need for discipline, is a concept of mind-blowing magnitude. When we accept this fact, we have moved off of "start" and can begin to really learn about life.

Moving off "start" takes faith. The more we learn in school, especially the sciences, the more the concept of a supreme creator will be challenged. A lot of very educated people have come to the conclusion that God is a figment of the human imagination, and they can make us feel simple and ashamed for accepting the faith of our families.

Don't make the mistake of equating advanced degrees with wisdom and understanding. At every stage in history there have been scientists on the cutting edge of "technology" who have believed in theories that later were found to be incorrect. And with time, it is likely that many of today's theories will be found to be, at best, only partially correct. We can waste a lot of life trying to figure out who is right and who is wrong to determine in the end that there are mysteries of the universe that no person can know. That time spent in ambiguity is time lost.

9

In academic study, we take advantage of the cumulative knowledge and discoveries of many brilliant minds over hundreds of years. We would not attempt to discover from scratch how to find the area of a circle or a parallelogram – we learn the formula that has already been discovered through someone else's work. Likewise, if we wanted to learn higher mathematics, we would not consult an English teacher but rather an expert in the field.

Apply the same common sense used in academic study to learning about life. Don't seek spiritual advice from someone with a Ph.D. in chemistry. Take advantage of the conclusions that the experts in philosophy and religion have drawn. Consult the great minds that are well-respected in our world today. Consult the great minds who have been influencing people for

Don't seek spiritual advice from someone with a Ph.D. in chemistry!

generations. Consult the ultimate authority on these matters, the one and only text book that has been in continual use for almost 2,000 years – the Bible. Begin the journey of life with the foregone conclusion that an awesome force of good, an all-knowing power is self-evident. This is fear of the Lord.

Hold this thought: I believe in God.

First, Let's Put My Parents in Their Place

Me and My Family: A Match Made in Heaven

Love Disguised as a Lecture

Mom, Dad, I Forgive You (Again and Again)   11

You Keep Talking but all I Hear Is… Good Advice

Me and My Family: A Match Made in Heaven

A wise daughter brings joy to her father, but a foolish daughter grief to her mother.

Proverbs 10:1

A wise daughter brings joy to her father, but a foolish woman despises her mother.

Proverbs 15:20

12 *She who brings trouble on her family will inherit only wind…*

Proverbs 11:29a

One of the hardest things about our walk with God is trying to make good decisions – how can we know if we're doing the right thing? That's why it's comforting to know that there is one thing in our lives that we had no power over and, therefore, we can be 100 percent certain is God's will for us: our parents. If they're kinda crazy, that can really mess with our heads. It may not make much sense right now, but God doesn't make mistakes, nor does God randomly dole out precious little souls to whoever happens to be the next in line. Our parents are who they are supposed to be – by divine order. Yes, even if we're adopted or an orphan.

Of all human relationships, the parent/child relationship is the most complex, the most perfect and the most problematic. Even highly introspective people are perplexed by the influence their children have on them and the wisest are, at times, confounded as to how to deal with certain parental situations. And no one can explain the love of a child for a parent; particularly that of a child who has been abused and abandoned yet continues to deeply love her estranged parent.

This mysterious and miraculous parent/child relationship is a great gift from God that can only be fully appreciated once we have played both roles in the relationship. Young women know half the story and can look forward to being completely blown away by the second half. The family bond is the most powerful that exists and the one that will sustain us throughout life like no friendship ever will.

And yet inherent in the parent/child relationship is a tug of war that can be seen as early as the terrible twos and continues unsatisfied until the child matures, defines herself, likes the result and begins to appreciate her parents' role in the person she has become.

13

Feelings that "my parents just don't get me" are common and natural and, to some extent, true. As we age, it seems we lose our ability to recall and relate to what life was like for us as children and teenagers. Just like a six-year-old can be incredibly annoying to a teenager – the teenager has forgotten she used to be just like that – parents forget what they were like as teens. Consequently, parents often expect much more from their children than they themselves ever were capable of.

On the other hand, it's frustrating for parents to put much love and effort into socializing and educating their children only to see the credit given to someone else. It always used to tweak my nose when someone would ask my daughter, "Where did you learn that," and she'd reply, "From TV," when I had taught her that same thing months or years earlier. The tendency to discount what parents have taught us intensifies through the teen years. We claim our successes as our very own, failing to acknowledge that almost everything non-academic that we know, we learned from our parents. In fact, we sometimes wonder

> Of all human relationships, the parent/child relationship is the most complex, the most perfect and the most problematic.

how *they* made it through life without *us*! How did they ever find their own keys, for example!

When I was in my early teens, one Sunday after dinner at the grandparents' house, I was a little sore about not being able to spend that day with my friends. I told my grandmother in a very sincere, inoffensive manner, "I love my friends more than my family." I really felt that way and for some years, I believed it. I think it is normal for a young person to prefer to be with people her own age over spending time with her parents and siblings. But those words haunt me now and I hope never to hear them from my own daughter.

14

A few decades later, friends have come and gone but who is still in my life? Who is there for me in the worst of times? My family. I have two wonderful friendships outside my family that have lasted about 20 years. I know what a true friend is and the unique and essential role they play as well.

Lucky for us, we don't have to choose between friends or family. We can have and love them both. There may be more times now that we prefer friends over family, but a time for appreciating family is coming around some day soon. Grab the opportunity to spend quality time with both.

Hold this thought: I love my family!

Love Disguised as a Lecture

My daughter, keep your father's commands and do not forsake your mother's teaching. Bind them upon your heart forever; fasten them around your neck. When you walk, they will guide you; when you sleep, they will watch over you; when you awake, they will speak to you.

Proverbs 6:20-22

At a certain stage in development – the teen years – we as young people look at our parents and wonder, "How did they make it this far in life without me?" We think there is nothing we can learn from these people, except maybe how *not* to live life. Our young minds have forgotten how we learned most of what we know. We are convinced our conscience must have spontaneously generated.

Yet even at this point, we have already become our parents – yikes! You know that little voice in our heads that says, "I better get out of bed now or I'll have to run to my class," – that's our parents' voice! That better judgment that holds our tongues when we feel like telling our boss where he can get off – our parents again. Appreciate the fact that for the first five years of our lives – years we cannot even remember – our parents were busy with constant prompting and instruction, laying the foundation for our conscience, common sense and good judgment.

Yet, parents can't teach us everything we need to know that early in life. Some things have to come a little later in life, such as advice on dating and choosing a spouse.

> We think there is nothing we can learn from these people, except maybe how not to live life. ... We are convinced our conscience must have spontaneously generated.

If we seal ourselves off from their influence just because they're geeks, we'll miss out on those late-teen, early twenties key lessons they still have to teach us.

We should be open to our parents' advice on these things. If we made it this far under their care, we can trust them to see us all the way through. We should soak up everything they have to say as if we were listening to a skydiving instructor in our one and only lesson before we have to jump out of the plane. We must pardon our parents if they aren't the best of instructors – if their instruction is laced with frustration or disguised as nagging. The very fact that they are bothering to argue with us or lecture us confirms one thing: they love us and they want the best for us.

From the security of our final years at home, we feel so certain of everything; life seems simple and we believe we will easily master life, love and business. Just as soon as the exhilarating sensation of being on our own wears off, the complexity of life will reveal itself and we will be glad to have "What would Mom do?" or "What would Dad do?" as a compass to guide us in decision-making.

Sadly, many young people do not have parents whose advice they can take. I'm not talking about nerdy parents or parents who never graduated from high school. I'm talking about truly unstable people who have been in and out of jail, have serious dysfunctional behavior such as drug and alcohol addictions, are mentally ill, or have abandoned their children completely. If that describes your parents and you are reading this book, I can assure you that God is taking care of you – perhaps through the concern of some adult in authority over you at school, a social services organization or even in jail. Or perhaps God is caring for you directly until He leads you to the protective umbrella of a mentor.

Whether we have a wonderful mom and dad to ask for advice,

parents we don't appreciate or no parents at all, all good advice is centered in the law of God. We can always ask God to show us the right way, watch over us while we sleep and speak clearly to us to keep us on the best path for our life.

"Then you will call, and the Lord will answer; you will cry for help, and he will say: Here I am" (Isaiah 58:9a).

Hold this thought: The good, the bad and the ugly: I have learned a lot from my parents.

17

Mom, Dad, I Forgive You (Again and Again)

If a woman curses her father or mother, her lamp will be snuffed out in pitch darkness.

Proverbs 20:20

The eye that mocks a father, that scorns obedience to a mother, will be pecked out by the ravens of the valley, will be eaten by vultures.

Proverbs 30:17

18

I think everyone has been mad enough at their mother and father to feel like cussing them out. And even if we didn't do it out loud, if we thought it, it's as good as having done it. Does this mean we'll be snuffed? I don't know for sure, but I understand the cursing in our proverb to mean something more significant, something we don't regret after an hour, something we hold in our hearts and keep on meaning for weeks, months and years. I understand this "curse" to mean a lasting disrespect or even a hatred for our parents.

Just to be sure, we might want to whisper a prayer of repentance for any disrespect we've shown our parents in the past and determine to relate to them in the future as God wills – with an attitude of respect and reverence. It's a variation on the same manner in which we relate to God Himself, and perhaps that's why this is such an important issue to God. If we can't respectfully relate to the ones who collaborated with God in our creation, the ones who we have physically present with us, how can we respect our ultimate Creator?

Whatever good, bad or ugly our parents may have done in our lifetime, we have them to thank for our life. As we know, they had a choice, and they decided to bring us into the world. If we have ever laughed, held a puppy, imagined a rabbit in the clouds or felt warm and tingly as we sank into a bathtub, at the very core of any of those experiences, we have our parents to thank.

This proverb isn't the only place in the Bible where we're advised to honor our father and mother – we see it throughout the scriptures. It is so important to God, in fact, that it made His short list – the Ten Commandments. In Old Testament times, people used to be stoned to death for disrespecting their parents, so strong was the prohibition. The message of the entire gospel is love and respect for other people, but why the emphasis on parents?

19

Could it be because God knows that parents can be some of the hardest people to honor and respect? God gave His people this law back in a day when it was acceptable in pagan religions for parents to offer their children as sacrifice to the gods. I just read in II Kings 6 about two women who made a pact to eat their sons to stay alive during a time of famine. You better believe God knows how pathetic some parents can be. And yet God commands us repeatedly to respect and honor them and strongly advises us of the eternal snuffing we'll get if we don't.

So, as a practical matter, how do we respect a pathetic parent? What's to respect? What about the parent who physically, sexually or emotionally abuses his or her children? What about the parent who is too high to see to it that her kids get a decent meal once a day? What about the parent who deserted his children in their infancy and has never lifted a finger since to fulfill his God-given parental obligations? These are hard cases, and I'm so sad to say, not uncommon.

First of all, we must understand that God will pronounce judgment on these parents. Jesus tells us that these parents would be better off if they tied a huge rock around their necks and jumped into the deep end of the ocean than to face what awaits them (Matthew 18:6). If we harbor resentment toward a parent who has abused or neglected us or someone we love, contemplate their future. Our just God will settle the account, of that we can be sure. That knowledge may help us let go of any feelings we have of wanting to even the score.

Even if we don't want to retaliate, we can still be holding on to hurt in the forms of anger and resentment. Remember the Lord's prayer, the one Jesus taught us to pray? In it there's the phrase, "Forgive us our sins, for we also forgive everyone who sins against us." In this prayer, Jesus also teaches us to ask for our "daily bread," which leads me to believe that Jesus intended us to pray something like this prayer every day.

20

We can use Jesus' prayer daily to renew our forgiveness and respect for our parents. We don't have to resolve to forgive our parents for their shortcomings for once and for all. All we have to do is resolve to forgive them today and make it stick for 24 hours. Then tomorrow, forgive them again. Pray, "Lord, forgive me my sins while I am here and now also forgiving those who have sinned against me." Before the 24 hours is up and we pray that prayer again, thoughts of anger and resentment toward our parents may attack us. When they come to our mind, we just say, "I have forgiven my parents." Even if we find ourselves 10 or 20 minutes into negative thought about them before it occurs to us to say it, reaffirm anyway: "I have forgiven my parents."

To be accurate, we are forgiving (the present progressive tense of the verb) our parents – meaning that daily we are in the active process of forgiving. Parents

> Parents who have poisoned the minds and souls of their children must be forgiven over and over again because the damage they've done continues to affect us. Even more so if our parents are still giving us grief.

who have poisoned the minds and souls of their children must be forgiven over and over, because the damage they've done continues to affect us. Even more so if our parents are still giving us grief. We may have to forgive our parents every day for the rest of our lives. We've got to do it – do whatever it takes to save ourselves from the eternal darkness that awaits those who harbor disrespect and resentment for their parents. And if eternity is too far off for us to care about, do it so we can have a happy life now. Does holding on to anger and resentment make for a better me?

If we're brimming over with anger, we probably cannot comprehend how a simple decision to stop being angry could possibly work. But it does, and we have nothing to lose in trying it. Just say to God right now, "Father, I forgive my parents and please work in my heart so that I may feel what I am saying." Every time we catch ourselves dwelling in anger and resentment, remember to say, "I have forgiven my parents."

Don't give up on this; your very existence depends on it.

Hold this thought: I have a basic respect for the two people who collaborated with God to make me.

You Keep Talking but all I Hear Is… Good Advice

Listen, my daughters, to a father's instruction; pay attention and gain understanding. I give you sound learning, so do not forsake my teaching. When I was a boy in my father's house, still tender, and an only child of my mother, he taught me and said, "Lay hold of my words with all your heart; keep my commands and you will live. Get wisdom, get understanding; do not forget my words or swerve from them. Do not forsake wisdom, and she will protect you; love her, and she will watch over you." Listen my daughter, accept what I say, and the years of your life will be many, … Hold on to instruction, do not let it go; guard it well, for it is your life. … My daughter, pay attention to what I say; listen closely to my words. Do not let them out of your sight, keep them within your heart.

Proverbs 4:1-6, 10, 13, 20-21

Is that not the mother of all lectures? Listen! Pay attention! Keep my commands! Get wisdom! Get understanding! Do not forget my words! And on and on! I can sympathize with Solomon as a boy – the lectures he must have sat through! In one Bible translation, the scripture says his father sat down and drilled him on these matters. As tedious as lectures can be, we know Solomon was actually a very lucky boy to have a father who cared so much about him that he would take time to instruct him.

When we are very young, lectures don't do us any good. We learn through hands-on, personal experience. As we grow and mature, we become able to learn in another way – through the experience of others – via lecture in school and advice from family and friends.

Learning through one's own experience is powerful and certainly preferred when it comes to learning about geography, cultures, languages and the arts. However, there is a whole other body of information that is far preferable to learn from other people's experience. Take mathematics, for example. Aren't we glad that someone else figured out for us that the circumference of a circle is equal to the diameter multiplied by π? When it comes to math, we want to take advantage of all that has already been discovered by someone else's experience and learn through lecture, without all the hassle and brainwork they had to endure. Then, with that foundation, we may move on to discover even greater things about math and how it relates to our lives and the physical universe.

"Life" is another subject in which we can greatly benefit from other people's experience. Yet many young women today reject the idea of taking advice from someone else about important decisions in life. They want to figure things out for themselves. This is about as sensible as setting out to discover again from scratch the circumference of a circle.

Imagine we're driving down the road and a red sports car passes us and speeds on ahead out of sight. Five minutes later, the car comes back toward us. The driver slows down and waves at us to stop. He hollers from his window, "The road is blocked up ahead. You won't be able to get through that way."

Do we reply: "Hey! This is my life and I'm going to live it the way I want to and if I make mistakes, well, it's nothing you haven't done too!" and then speed on ignoring the other driver's advice? Surely, we wouldn't do something so silly. But if we have ever invoked the "It's my life, I'll make my own mistakes" mantra in response to good advice from someone who cares about us, we've done something just that foolish.

That "my life" mantra, or rebel's yell, usually follows advice we don't want to hear. Our parent, teacher, mentor or friend is telling us that we are about to do something we'll regret. It's obvious to everyone and we know it as well, but our course is set and we are determined the outcome of our actions will be different than what everyone predicts.

At these times, when our desires pit us against common sense and the wise counsel of friends and family, instead of insisting on driving down that road ourselves to find that the road is indeed blocked, try this: say, "I appreciate your concern. I'll give that some thought." That's so easy! We've just averted a conflict and prolonged lecture, we haven't committed ourselves to any change in course and we're in a great position: we can do anything from here and we won't have to eat our words. Instead of backing ourselves into a corner with a rebellious retort, we've created an open field and we can go anywhere we want without looking or feeling like we're giving in. We *are* making our own choices!

Next, we should do what we said we would do: give it some thought. Our head and heart will be clear to consider the advice because we're not in conflict with the person giving it. Will that advice save us a wasted trip down a blocked road? Proverbs 27:12 says, "The prudent see danger and take refuge, but the simple keep going and suffer for it."

Hold this thought: I learn from the mistakes of others, not repeat them.

chapter two

Owner of a Lonely Heart

I Was the Frog in the Frying Pan

I Did It My Way…and Totally Flopped!

Love Feast: All You Can Eat   25

Oh, to be Like Thee, Noble Civic!

No Peeing in the Pool Allowed

Make Your Cake and Eat It Too

I Give You My Heart
Used, Broken, Battered and Worn

It's a Biological Thang

The Helpful Green-Eyed Monster

A Cinderella Story

I Was the Frog in the Frying Pan

The lips of an adulteress drip honey and her speech is smoother than oil; but in the end she is bitter as gall, sharp as a double-edged sword. Her feet go down to death; her steps lead straight to the grave. She gives no thought to the way of life; her paths are crooked, but she knows it not.

Proverbs 5:3-6

26

…for a prostitute is a deep pit and a wayward wife is a narrow well. Like a bandit she lies in wait, and multiplies the unfaithful among men.

Proverbs 23:27-28

Reading the many warnings against loose women in the Proverbs could give a woman an inferiority complex. The woman always seems to be the "bad guy" – the seductress that lays a trap for innocent young men. Don't let that get you down – it's just allegory, a writing tool to help people get the point. And that point is that sin is a seductress and today it is trapping young men and women in much the same way. The adulteress is a symbol that represents the sin of promiscuity, or sex outside of marriage. Don't take it personally that Solomon used a woman to be the bad guy throughout these lessons on promiscuity. He evens the score by portraying wisdom as a woman too.

   As we read the Proverbs in this book, we will often reverse the gender choices Solomon made and understand that these teachings against sex outside of marriage apply equally to women and men. Today women are as able to sleep around as men are. There is still more stigma attached to a woman's promiscuity, but feminine promiscuity is clearly widely acceptable. The standard in movies and television is sex by the third date, if not on the first! This may not reflect our reality, but the rock-bottom standards the media portrays as "normal," along with pressure from peers and our culture in general, are worming away at our resolve and higher standards even now.

In Solomon's day and right up until about a hundred years ago, when a person married early in life, sex before marriage was probably just as tempting, but certainly not as accessible. Most cultures had strong prohibitions on sex before marriage. For the few years a woman was eligible for courtship, dates were few, if any, and highly structured. Sex before marriage was a scandalous departure from the norm – particularly for a woman.

In the past 100 years, this aspect of our society has taken a 180-degree turn. Now young people are encouraged to wait until they are much older to marry – even into their 30s. Dating starts at about the same age it did centuries ago, but it lasts a lot longer, sometimes decades. Sex before marriage is the norm and marrying as a virgin is the almost unbelievable exception. Men and women alike are encouraged to "sow their wild oats" and "get it out of their system" before they marry so that they can be faithful and satisfied when they finally marry.

Yet infidelity and divorce statistics are alarmingly high, indicating that "getting it out of our system" clearly does not work. Apparently, what happens instead is that restlessness in the dating years creates patterns that continue after the initial novelty of marriage has worn off. The disastrous consequences of our new norm range from rampant sexually transmitted diseases and other women's health problems to children without fathers, 1.5 million abortions annually (in the United States alone), and a cheapening of the sexual experience that was meant to bond a man and woman in marriage. This, in turn, results in high rates of divorce and infidelity, disintegrating the family unit and leading to a whole other list of woes including juvenile delinquency and higher crime against women.

Why does society not recognize how detrimental our new

27

norm is? Because this crooked path is coated with honey. We may have had the experience before of eating something delicious that later made us very sick. It's the same with sex before marriage. Sex is good. It is a gift from God and certainly enjoyable; comparing it to honey is quite accurate. But sex outside of marriage is like that delicious meal that we so enjoy, not realizing it is swarming with salmonella microorganisms. Just as poisoned food can taste very good but will surely leave us in pain, abusing the gift of sex feels great while it's happening but will make us regrettably sick later on, as the experience digests itself in our life and soul.

28

Unlike food poisoning however, the lag time between sex and its ill-effects makes it difficult to trace the negative consequences back to the error that caused them. This extreme disconnect is the only explanation I can see for why so many people would enthusiastically engage in an activity from which no good can come. Sometimes the incubation period of negative consequences is a matter of years, such as in the case of AIDS or the woman who finds out she needs a surgery to remove cancerous cells from her cervix – one consequence of too many sex partners. Other negative consequences are so prevalent that we have accepted them as normal. It is not until we experience them ourselves that we recognize the very real pain and regret involved in each abortion, in raising a child without a father, in a divorce and in infidelity. These trials that fictional characters on television go through and get over in one episode take years and many tears to resolve in real life.

Of course, the way to avoid all this heartache is to remain pure until marriage. The only problem with that is how very difficult it is in the world today. It's like going to Golden Corral on an empty stomach and having nothing but a cup of tea!

Marrying earlier in life certainly shortens our exposure to the temptation of sex before marriage, but it is hardly advisable. God may have it in His plan for us to marry young, but it is not within our control to determine when we will meet our true love and marry. Love is not an event we can schedule. Besides that, there are very few young people equipped to survive an early marriage.

The same forces causing young people to wait until their 20s and 30s to marry are slowing down social maturity in other ways too. We have traded social and emotional development for higher education in the sciences and humanities. Two centuries ago, by age 18, most teens had learned the skills needed to successfully run a family. Today, we don't focus on those skills; we focus on education, career-skills and how to succeed in business and the community. Even if a young person has the 19th-century skill set, in general, he or she does not qualify for jobs that pay well enough to sustain a family today. Without the social and emotional tools and financial resources needed to succeed in marriage, the chance for a successful marriage is slim.

Don't believe yourself to be an exception and think you can beat the odds and have a successful marriage from the age of 18 or 19. I'm about to give you a hard pill to swallow, and if you don't believe me, research it on your own (see Bibliography): Thinking you can overcome the odds where others have not is typical teenage thinking. One of the hallmarks of the brain's last stage of development in the late teen years is a feeling and belief that you can succeed at anything. This blind optimism aids the emerging adult to integrate into society – where great things are at work already – without feeling insignificant or overwhelmed. That same survival optimism can fool us into believing that somehow we have achieved a level of maturity our same-age peers have not. Even if we and our spouse had all the maturity and resources we needed to succeed in marriage, we still live in a time and culture that is completely hostile to marriage at an early age.

So what's a gal to do? We probably shouldn't marry young;

holding out is next to impossible… Help!

There's no sugar-coating it. Remaining pure is one of the most difficult tasks for any young adult. Sex is the devil's most successful lure of our times and even many Christians, recognizing the mismatch between the expectations of purity and our entire culture, have rationalized a compromise, which is, of course, also a victory for Satan.

God's one will for our life in this matter is purity until marriage.

Yes, this *is* possible but only through total nonconformity – actually, all-out rebellion – against the societal norm on dating, physical contact and sex. Want to be a rebel with a cause? Here's a good one.

If we are already sexually active, God's will is that we refrain from further self-destructive sex. Regaining purity is more of a challenge than maintaining purity but can be done. Satan will infiltrate our mind and tell us that we're just drawing lines in the sand, we've already done it and there's no harm in doing it again, particularly if it is with the same person and even more particularly if we plan to marry this person. Those are very effective lies. I repeat: God's will is that we refrain from further self-destructive sex.

OK, OK – but I for one am tired of hearing this without getting any practical suggestions on how to go about it! Here are some nitty-gritty strategies for all-out rebellion against premarital sex, whether we're holding out for marriage or resolved to refrain from further sex.

Set firm boundaries for being with the opposite sex, particularly in a dating relationship. I recommend the following: 1. Stay upright at all times when you are alone with your boyfriend. 2. Allow your boyfriend to touch only parts of your body that would be exposed if you were wearing shorts (not short shorts!) and a t-shirt. Do not allow your "shorts and t-shirt zone" to be touched even through clothing, except for your "pat-on-the-back zone."

A couple of good strategies to help maintain these boundaries are dating in groups and having an accountability buddy:
1. Time alone with a boyfriend is time you can expect to be tempted. Try to always stay in public or have a friend around. To get to know your boyfriend in ways he cannot express in group situations, spend time talking on the phone or on IM.
2. Share your desire to stay pure with one close friend and ask that person to help. Promise to always be honest with her and tell her if you do cross a boundary. In advance, tell her some things that will help to motivate you to keep your purity goal if your resolve starts to weaken.

31

Hold yourself accountable by writing yourself a letter. Do it now while you feel confident and full of faith that you can remain pure. List all the reasons why purity is important to you. Write convincingly about your present clarity of mind and purpose. Say things to yourself that can jolt you back on track should you start to lose perspective. Give the letter to your accountability buddy and ask her to present it to you if she feels you need it.

Why do we need an accountability buddy? Notice the end of our proverb: "...her paths are crooked, but she knows it not." If we give in to temptation, we cannot count on our own ability to realize we have erred. A faithful accountability buddy *can* tell us when we've taken a wrong turn. And when that time comes, we must trust that person in the same way we trusted her on the day she became our accountability buddy. We're not going to

Even many Christians, recognizing the mismatch between the expectations of purity and our entire culture, have rationalized a compromise, which is, of course, also a victory for Satan.

believe we're on the wrong path. It will *feel* wrong to stop, turn around and go back in the other direction. We mustn't trust our own sense of direction in these times. Trust the buddy; trust the clarity of mind we had on the day we wrote ourselves that letter; trust in God's perfect will for our life – That perfect will is now, and always will be, to remain pure until marriage.

The key to success in this endeavor is never to cross our boundaries – at all, ever! If we should, we will find it is the first step on a slippery slope; one broken boundary will lead to another and another until our resolve is completely undone.

32 Don't let that happen. Maintaining our boundaries requires the triumph of mind over matter – it's a mental discipline and no one else can do this for us. Nonetheless, don't go it alone because we can't succeed that way either. We are fighting against forces of evil that want to poison our life. Fight back – not with might, not with power, but with the Spirit of God. Call on God's power every day to help remain pure. Call on God before every date. Call on God when the boyfriend is walking us to the door. Call on God when he wants to come in. Call on God when he doesn't want to stop at our boundary line. The Spirit of God will rise up behind us like a wall to keep that boundary firm.

Sex outside of marriage is a sin that separates us from God. When we lose our resolve and begin to cross our boundaries, if we would take the time to reflect on our spiritual life, we would see that our slide down the slippery slope corresponds to a weakening of our faith. We have questions we didn't have before and doubts about God and whether there even is a divine will for us. We spend less time on our relationship with God – it's

I had high expectations of remaining pure until marriage. I went off to college with them and there, very slowly, my resolve wore thin until there was nothing left of it.

crowded out by constant activity and a barely perceptible cha-otic feeling. All this is because it is simply not possible to allow sex as our one exception to a healthy relationship with God. Sex outside of marriage is the one bad apple that will rot the whole barrel.

OK, so I've made my point, right? How many ways can I say, "Stay pure!" I hope you don't feel like I'm preaching at you, be-cause that is *not* what this is. I'm the guy who is hollering, "The road is blocked up ahead. You won't be able to get through that way."

Remember him – he knows what the conditions of the road are because he just came from that direction. I am sharing les-sons with you that I have learned through my experiences, regrettably. I had high expectations of remaining pure until marriage. I went off to college with them and there, very slowly, my resolve wore thin until there was nothing left of it.

They say if you place a frog in a frying pan and put the pan over a fire, the frog will not jump out, but will sit there and heat up until it has cooked to death. The frog adjusts to the warmth of its environment, never realizing it is becoming dangerous to the point of death. I was that frog in the frying pan. I was so slowly violating my boundaries that I had no perspective of be-ing in a downward spiraling motion. And when I lost all resolve and began having sex, my life was too fun and busy to stop and contemplate what I had done and where I was going. I recall a vague feeling of knowing I was doing wrong, but Satan had control of my conscious thought and had my vision locked-in on the good times.

I had a lot of "good times" and the consequences of those times have been the greatest heartaches in my life. Among many other regrettable things, I brought a child into this world without a father to guide her through life. From outside ap-pearances, you would never know how much we both have suffered because of it. God is gracious and has protected and

33

blessed that child in the way He cares for orphans and widows. And like an eagle swooping down and rescuing a fallen chick, God picked me up off the wrong path very quickly and set me back down on the right one. I'm very content now to stay under His wing of protection and guidance.

I pray that maintaining your purity will be your goal and your achievement. It requires much attention because it is Satan's favorite trap of our times. With the same caution with which we lock our doors at night, we need to beware of attacks on our purity – before and after marriage. It is a new challenge each day. Each day, call on the Spirit of God to make you the winner.

Hold this thought: I can do all things – even stay pure until marriage – through Christ who gives me strength.

I Did It My Way…and Totally Flopped!

To a woman belongs the plans of the heart, but from the Lord comes the reply of the tongue. All a woman's ways seem innocent to her, but motives are weighed by the Lord. Commit to the Lord whatever you do, and your plans will succeed. The Lord works everything out for his own ends – even the wicked for a day of disaster.

Proverbs 16:1-4

When I was a teenager, I wanted to get married and start a family by the time I was 19. When I finally got to that ripe old age, I had other plans. I was in college and determined to get a degree. I wanted a career with part of my heart and the other part wanted to find love and get married. I still had a family plan, it just started after college, during which time I'd meet the man I would marry.

I had it all figured out, except for one thing. I didn't realize we can't plan when we'll marry. We can plan a wedding, but we can't put "fall in love, date one year and get married" on our calendar. Those things are of God and I don't think God likes when we try to tamper with them.

If we long for a family, first of all, we shouldn't feel badly about that. Today, an immature women's liberation movement would make us feel as though that is a lesser goal in life. That is not true. A loving family is an ultimate goal in life for women and men. Everyone wants it and that's a fact. Not everyone defines family the same way – some people don't want children, some want a lifelong mate without legal entanglements, but we all want to love and be loved and that's the same as wanting a family.

Secondly, the great thing about wanting a family is that it is not mutually exclusive – we can have a lot of other goals right along with our goals to have a loving family. Most of the successful men and women in history had families. The fact of the matter is that most people either are married or have been married. And yet business goes on as usual. People can get things done with a spouse and kids. We shouldn't let anyone make us feel old-fashioned or conservative because we want to get married.

So we have the green light for a family, now we just need to find that perfect man, date for a while and tie the knot. Nice idea, but is it what God has planned for us at this time? Maybe. Maybe not.

God can see right down into places in our heart and soul that we don't even know exist and God sees if we want a family for healthy reasons or for unhealthy reasons. If our desire to have a family stems from some need or dysfunction in our lives, God may want us to work on that – to grow and develop and become better people so that we conquer the dysfunction in our lives and bring a healthy person to our marriage relationship.

God can speak planets into existence, yet despite that great power, God rarely forces Himself on us. God bids and urges and beckons and calls and opens doors and closes doors to lead His children along in life. It is entirely possible to ignore those bids, calls and open doors and take a crow bar and force open a closed door. It's incredibly foolish, but entirely possible.

Tired of being single? Yes, we can marry on our timeline the person we deem right without regard to God's plan for us in the matter. But what are we inviting on ourselves?

An immature women's liberation movement would make us feel as though that is a lesser goal.

Think of a time you failed because you did something foolish – you stayed up too late watching movies and then were late to work and received a reprimand. You blew off studying for a test and got a bad grade. Take the humiliation and defeat you felt at a small failure and multiply it times 10,000 in intensity and length of time it wears on you. That begins to describe a failed marriage. You don't want that for yourself, do you?

The way to avoid that disaster is to commit ourselves to God. Tell God, "I'll do whatever you want me to do in life, Father. Show me clearly what that is. Swing the doors wide open and I'll walk through them." When we take this approach in earnest, not just as a daily mantra, but as a sincere desire for our life, two great things happen: 1. The plans of our heart align with God's plan for our life; and 2. Our plans succeed.

37

Last night I heard a nine-year-old girl singing a popular song with lyrics including "my life," "I decide," and "I'll do it my way." That self-centered strategy is pop poison to a young woman's soul. This is the life God gave us (and can take away at any moment). Let God decide – because God is so much better at it than we are – God's view is from above the maze, unlike our limited perspective from inside the maze. If we do it the way God wants us to, we won't be singing the blues later for having done it our way.

Hold this thought: I plan to do what God wants me to do in life. That way, I can't fail.

on my own now

Love Feast: All You Can Eat

Let love and faithfulness never leave you; bind them around your neck, write them on the tablet of your heart. Then you will win favor and a good name in the sight of God and man.

Proverbs 3:3-4

Regardless of who we are, even if we try to avoid love by taking a vow to marry the church, like a nun does, we will be hurt by love at some point. Even the most faithful of lovers and husbands will say or do something at some point that will rip right into our heart. Some of us are hurt by love because it eludes us. The message in this proverb is that despite what love brings (or doesn't bring), we should hold on to the hope of love.

We all probably know someone who has had a bad relationship and break up and has sworn off of love completely. "I'll never fall in love again. I've been hurt too badly and I just can't go through that again." What a sad person. God wants us to keep our hearts open to the possibility of love – keep the faith that we can love again. A faith in love will make us a beautiful person – actually attractive to others and to the very type of man with which we can have a great love.

This doesn't mean that we should chase after romance the way a puppy will follow whoever calls it. Even when we were babies we knew better than to go into the welcoming arms of just anyone. We had discrimination and discernment then, and we have it now. Let's use it. We must have a standard for ourselves, but not based on worldly things like: must have a car; must have a job; must like the Beatles; must wear Abercrombie. Instead, the standard should be based on the important things like: must be respectful of others and show respect to me; must believe in God; must be law-abiding... "What about looks," you say? God knows our taste better than we do! God knows what we will find attractive today and still at age 45. When we ask God to bring us a man, our love will not only meet our standards, he will be *HOT!*

A longing in our heart for a great love is a good thing. It means we have hope for love. Waiting patiently on God's perfect timing can be difficult. Here's where the faith comes in. We must have faith that God is crafting just the right relationship for us. Think of the love God is preparing as a feast. God is busy cooking right now. Sure, we are hungry now and we feel the pain of that hunger. But God is in love's kitchen slaving away, and something delicious is coming our way very soon – we can be sure of it! If we have faith that God is cooking up a great love, it will help us resist snacking before our meal comes along.

Just like snacking can spoil an appetite for a delicious dinner, getting into many errant relationships can spoil our appetite for the love God intends for us – especially if some of those relationships are rotten. If we try this one and that one and each of them leaves a bad taste in our mouth, will we be predisposed to try a taste of the relationship God has worked so hard to prepare? We've had so many bad ones, we'll be afraid of (or maybe automatically reject) the good one when it comes along.

I'm not ready to say that God intends us to only date one person. God may have several important relationships for us – relationships in which we learn valuable lessons that help to refine our personality and prepare us to be successful in marriage.

Even when our hearts get broken or it seems we will never find anyone to love, we must embrace love all the same. We shouldn't let the waiting make us jaded

> Even the most faithful of lovers and husbands will say or do something at some point that will rip right into our heart.

or bitter. Let's have faith that God's true love for our life is on its way and open our hearts to all the possibilities. God's love for us could be waiting in the form of an orphaned child that needs a single mother or an elderly person that needs our care. If we wait in hope of love, full of faith, God will lay out a feast of love so satisfying that we will never be hungry again.

Hold this thought: God is preparing the perfect love for me.

Oh, to be Like Thee, Noble Civic!

A wife of noble character is her husband's crown, but a disgraceful wife is like decay in his bones.

Proverbs 12:4

He who finds a wife finds what is good and receives favor from the Lord.

Proverbs 18:22

House and wealth are inherited from parents, but a prudent wife is from the Lord.

Proverbs 19:14

Do you have the makings of a good wife? How about a good doctor, manager or customer service representative? Whatever we're planning on becoming someday, we should begin now to prepare ourselves.

Hang with me for a few paragraphs because I admit this is a pathetic analogy, but finding a spouse can be a lot like buying a car. When we first learn to drive, we want that dream car right off the bat, but we can't have it. Unless we're a rich brat, Daddy's not going to buy us a Corvette. We simply have to settle for something that is a lot less expensive, but still has an edge.

Nonetheless, we dream of that perfect car – for me, it was the Jaguar XJ6. We practically get whiplash gawking when we see one drive by. We daydream scenarios in which we can afford our dream car. We say, "When I get my student loans paid off, that's what I'll buy to celebrate."

Time passes, we mature and learn more about price and availability of parts, consumer reports and gas mileage; we begin to appreciate trunk space and leg room and even a color that doesn't show dirt. And most of all, we learn how much we can afford to pay each month on a car.

Then the time comes; we are ready to buy our first brand new car. At this intersection of reality, we give up our dream car. We still love the idea of it, but we realize that it's not practical – the maintenance and money required are too much. What we're looking for now is value and reliability – a car we can trust, a car we can grow old(er) with. What looks good now are Chryslers, Fords, Hondas, Nissans and Toyotas.

And all of those are fine choices – the owner will be satisfied for the life of the car!

As young women, we'd all like to be a Mercedes, Lamborghini or Rolls Royce, and it bums us out as we realize we are more like a Honda Civic. But you know what? A Honda Civic is a great car! And what makes it great is that when you turn the key in the morning – hot or cold – year after year, it starts right up. When it's time to purchase tires, they're not $200 a pop. You can find your air filter in Wal-Mart! When you buy a Honda Civic you can be sure of many years together. Honda Civic is good; it is noble and it is prudent. The "noble character" mentioned in our first proverb does not refer to a royal blood line like a Rolls, but rather reliability, trustworthiness and industriousness – virtues of a Honda Civic.

How about us? Can we be counted on to be honest always and remain true to a life-long commitment? Will we pull our weight in the family by working as hard as we can, doing the best job possible to make our family successful? That's noble.

> As young women, we'd all like to be a Mercedes, Lamborghini or Rolls Royce, and it bums us out as we realize we are more like a Honda Civic.

Will we be our man's personal cheerleader, keep his weaknesses to ourselves and promote him like a political candidate? Will we weigh our words and every major decision to make sure they are reasonable and fair? That's prudent.

And those are the things that matter to any man worth marrying.

When we're single, married life is hypothetical and it's impossible to say what we'd do in a hypothetical situation – to declare with certainty what kind of wife we'll be. However, one old piece of marital advice rings true here: You can't marry expecting a person to change. And that applies to us, too. If we are not already developing a noble and prudent character, walking down the aisle won't magically transform us. A Lamborghini cannot become a Honda Civic on the day it is driven off the lot. A Honda Civic has to be built and developed over time with the specific intention of becoming a car known for its value, quality, reliability and low maintenance.

43

Are we investing our time and resources into developing a Lamborghini – with trademark perfect manicure, pedicure and waxed legs? Or are we becoming a noble Civic, using our time and resources to become a woman of character? Our successful marriage begins now by developing the noble and prudent character that will make us good wives, "a real find" and a crown for our future husband.

Hold this thought: I can work on my marriage even while I'm single.

No Peeing in the Pool Allowed

Above all else, guard your heart, for it is the wellspring of life.
Proverbs 4:23

Now this sounds like some very good advice, but as a practical matter, how do you guard your heart? Perhaps we first need to figure out what we're guarding ourselves against.

In this scripture, Solomon uses the analogy of our heart as a wellspring – the source of our life's drinking water – something vital to survival. A healthy heart puts out clean drinking water. A broken heart, a sick heart, a jaded heart, a bitter heart all pollute the water that springs from it. When we have a heartache, we are metaphorically drinking dirty water. We can drink this contaminated water for some time before it makes us sick; but count on it, it will make us sick.

How did the water get dirty? Someone walked right up to the edge of our wellspring and dumped garbage in it. How did this litterer get in? Well, the same way anyone gets in – we let him in. Only we can allow access to the source of our life's water – our heart.

Think about a heartache you had once. What caused it? I can think of many things that affect my emotions, spirit and even my soul, but only two things cause my heart to really get that crushing feeling in my chest as though I am sick at heart: betrayal/disappointment by someone I trusted too much, and love lost.

Lost love can happen in a number of ways which cannot be prevented – the most tragic of which is death. Losing loved ones to death will heal over much time and by asking God to pour out a comforting balm on our wounded heart. Embrace the heartache of lost love by death. This pain, like the pruning of a rose, can produce a much bigger, stronger heart. Jesus said,

"Blessed are those who mourn" (Matthew 5:4).

Betrayal and disappointment, on the other h
the heart. After this garbage is dumped on us, we
bitter and jaded. We may build walls so high arou
that not even true love can enter. Or, it can cause us to give up trying to guard our heart at all and resign ourselves to being a dumping ground for any garbage that comes our way.

Guarding our heart, in practical terms, is trusting and becoming intimate friends only with people we have observed over a long period of time to be truly trustworthy. We let our guard down when we become intimate with someone, either physically or emotionally. This person now has access to our heart – our life's drinking water, our wellspring. When we become intimate with someone we hardly know or someone who is not trustworthy, we open our wellspring to possible pollution.

Guarding our heart is so important in a culture that wants us to believe in love at first sight. Movies and television promote instant intimacy and sex on the first date. What they don't show is the real-life damage that "instant intimacy" does to our hearts after the romance is gone.

Many people have difficulty guarding their hearts. Some are too naively trusting, instantly befriending anyone who seems pleasant. Others who have suffered extreme hurt, such as an abused young woman, so desperately want to be loved that they make an amusement park out of the sacred grounds around their heart. "Come one, come all! Drink, swim, water ski, even pee in the springs – I don't care, just be with me." How sad.

Sadder still is that the person who accepts this kind of amusement park invitation is generally the type of person who *will* pee in the water. And so it is that the innocent and those most in need of love and trust, those who fling open their guard gates and welcome all who pass by, attract the flotsam and jetsam of life.

Realizing that we are a special child of God should cause us to want to guard our heart. When we see ourselves as children of the King, we understand how precious we are and we begin to love ourselves and respect ourselves enough to keep up the guard around our heart and preserve it as a pure wellspring that produces clean drinking water.

Don't let just anyone have access to your heart! God never intended us to be intimate with a lot of people and by no means with people we hardly know. If our life's drinking water is already filthy from all the debris of past relationships, it is not too late to start a clean-up project.

Here's what to do: become very selective about who you trust with your deepest thoughts, your secrets and your body. If you have loving, supportive parents, you should include one or both of them in this most intimate circle of loved ones. A friend should only be allowed after she has been tried and found true with smaller tests of confidence. This takes time – time to determine if she will defend you to others when you are not around, if she will hold in confidence your embarrassments and disappointments, and if she will be physically present when you need her there to support you. Throughout your life, keep the number of people you grant access small and manageable – two or three special guests is plenty. Allow a family member, a dear friend and finally, a special man to slowly approach and enter your heart.

> Time is an essential factor in knowing if a person is worthy of our heart's trust. We may be able to eliminate some people quickly, but there is no shortcut to qualify a person as trustworthy.

Time is an essential factor in knowing if a person is worthy of our heart's trust. We may be able to eliminate some people quickly, but there is no shortcut to qualify a person as trustworthy. In my experience, it takes a minimum (and again I say *minimum*) of six months of consistent contact to get past the introductory phase of a new friendship or relationship. Only after this time can you *begin* to evenly and accurately evaluate a new relationship.

Rushing intimacy has disastrous consequences for even the best judges of character. Take your time. Guard your heart.

Hold this thought: I will not try to rush intimacy.

47

Make Your Cake and Eat It Too

If a woman digs a pit, she will fall into it; if a woman rolls a stone, it will roll back on her.

Proverbs 26:27

I hope by now you're getting the hang of extrapolating the meaning of proverbs. The above proverb is not a verse for ditch diggers and quarry workers. This verse holds a truth for every living person that I can sum up in one word: consequences.

You've baked a cake before, haven't you? Have you ever baked one from scratch? A few more ingredients are needed than the boxed mix, eggs and water. Starting from scratch we'll need flour, sugar, butter or oil, eggs, baking powder, salt and maybe a few more ingredients depending on what kind of cake we're making. When we put all of that in a bowl and mix it up and then put it in the hot oven for a period of time, what comes out is a cake. It's not rocket science, it's culinary science. We have a formula (recipe) and a process (baking) that create a desired result (cake).

What happens if we forget an ingredient? Will our cake be a success without flour? How about without sugar? Even if we leave out the small essential ingredients, the salt and the baking powder, the cake will flop. OK, it is possible to do without eggs, if you substitute something that has the same effect – like buttermilk and baking soda. We cannot, however, ignore the egg altogether. We have to have all the essential ingredients listed above.

What's not terribly important is the order in which we add them to the bowl, how long we mix them, what shape pan we use – we can even use a cookie sheet – and we still get a yummy treat. There's room for variation in this formula, but just not in the essential ingredients. In fact, the possibilities are infinite – from red velvet cake to hummingbird cake to pine-apple upside down cake to carrot cake to German chocolate cake and beyond – the essential ingredients for cake are like the notes in a musical scale from which unlimited symphonies can be created.

You know all of this about cake – I've not taught you anything new – if you want to end up with cake you have to use the right ingredients. No arguments, right? Would you then agree that the same is true about anything we're cooking up in our life? If we want to achieve a desired result, we have to start with the essential ingredients for that recipe.

Let's look at the recipe for a successful marriage:

One godly, mature man
One godly, mature woman
A good measure of time to get to know each other
Two whole purities
A blessing from the parents (or caring adults in our lives)
Financial resources sufficient to support a family

If we put all these ingredients together, we've got a great marriage. Did you notice something missing in that recipe? There's no love! What kind of marriage can you make without love? Some would argue that love is a byproduct of a success-ful marriage. For most of human history, there's been no love between the bride and groom on the wedding day, but it was expected that love would grow as byproduct of a successful marriage.

What happens if we substitute one dysfunctional man for one godly, mature man? We'll be cooking up trouble, not a success-ful marriage. The same is true if we substitute a dysfunctional woman for the godly, mature woman, or if we substitute a godly immature woman for a godly, mature woman. If we have grown up in a dysfunctional family, we may need to take some years to rehabilitate ourselves into functional women before we can be one of the essential ingredients in a successful marriage. If we're young and immature (and the two generally go hand in hand), we need to wait until we've matured to become one of the essential ingredients in a successful marriage.

What about the blessing of the parents or the caring adult in our life? Is that really important? Can't we substitute the blessing of friends instead? Well, if you're 50 years old and your parents are in a nursing home with Alzheimer's, sure, friends will work in that sort of a pinch. But when parents or the caring adult in our lives are able to give the blessing, we can't leave them out of the recipe and get a successful marriage.

You were with me all through that cake baking thing, weren't you? How about through the recipe for a successful marriage? Are you still with me or are you starting to disagree with this baking analogy?

You know, you can disagree all you want, but that doesn't change the recipe for a successful marriage. Just like we can try repeatedly to bake a cake without the essential ingredients, so too, we can try marriage over and over, leaving out essential ingredients. Either way the result will be inevitable: it'll leave a bad taste in our mouth. At the end of the day, our kitchen is a disaster when we experiment with cake recipes. When we experiment with the recipe for a successful marriage, our life becomes a disaster. Before we know it, we're 30 years old and divorced! How did this happen we wonder? We need to go back and read the

> Can't we substitute the blessing of friends instead? Well, if you're 50 years old and your parents are in a nursing home with Alzheimer's, sure, friends will work in that sort of a pinch.

recipe and see which ingredient we forgot or where we tried to make a substitution.

Why don't we just follow the recipe to begin with? Do we think that at the ripe old age of 18, 19, 20 or just a little older we can shortcut a process that's ordained by God and get a new result? Do we know better than the wisdom of the ages?

When we throw a bunch of substitute ingredients in a bowl and mix them together, we will get exactly what we have made – gunk. God loves us and forgives our sin, but God seldom performs miracles in the oven. Though the guilt for our foolishness is washed away in the cleansing tide of Christ's blood, we still get the cake we made and we have to eat it too.

Hold this thought: If I want cake, I have to use the right ingredients.

I Give You My Heart
Used, Broken, Battered and Worn

Many a woman claims to have an unfailing love, but a faithful woman who can find?
Who can say, "I have kept my heart pure; I am clean and without sin"?

Proverbs 20:6, 9

I got married at the ripe old age of 37. Some may say I was wise to have waited as long as I did. Though I never intended to be quite that old at the altar, throughout my 20s, I felt proud for not having married young and instead having completed my education and made a few strides in a career.

When I finally chose a husband, I had a sense of certainty about it based on a couple of things. First, I believed God had sent him my way because just weeks before we started to date, I had asked for a husband in earnest – with all of my heart. I had prayed for God to prepare a husband for me many times before, though never fully wanting him to come along just yet. However, when I prayed that time just after my 36th birthday, I was truly finished with dating and wanted to be settled.

The other factor that gave me certainty in marrying was that I knew I was making an informed choice. Unlike the high school sweethearts that end up a happily married couple with absolutely no basis of comparison, I had a wide basis of comparison. Through two-plus decades and very many romances, I had pinpointed the exact qualities I knew to be important for a successful relationship for me.

That list of qualities I had in my mid 30s was quite different than it had been in my late teens. When I was young, I wanted a man who was: drop-dead gorgeous with a razor-sharp wit, intelligent, ambitious and could sing. With criteria like this, it may come as no surprise that I used to eliminate men based on the type of shoes they wore. Wow! Now that's shallow.

I'm not sure when exactly I stopped paying attention to the shoes (probably when I resorted to buying Payless brand myself out of financial necessity), but I do remember when I finally realized that my criteria were bogus. It was when I met the man who fit it all completely. In addition to being everything I thought I wanted, he had dimples!

And you know what else? He was addicted to prescription pain killers, alcohol, marijuana, was a compulsive liar, diagnosed manic/depressive and had fathered five babies, all of whom had been aborted on his urgings. Amazing that one person can be all that, isn't it – all the wonderful things I had in mind, plus a few more I didn't mention, and all those awful things, plus a few more I didn't mention! That man changed my life – big time! A relationship with him revealed to me what is really important – honesty, loyalty and mental health!

53

I eventually found those good qualities in the man I married, and so went face forward to the altar, never looking back or around to see if perhaps there was something I was missing before tying the knot. My years of dating had resulted in a thorough knowledge of what's available and I knew then and still know now, that I had "a keeper."

That's a comfort to me and will be an important factor in the success of my relationship. With God's help, I will always be a faithful wife because I know that I can't do better than what I have and not even drop-dead gorgeous is worth jeopardizing the relationship it took me the larger part of my life to find.

As a result of growing up in a dysfunctional family, and out of some basic immaturity, I had shallow and errant criteria for selecting a husband. I thank God that my life experience reshaped my ideas of what makes a good husband to a more value-based set of criteria. I needed that time as a single person to work on me, to change my dysfunctional thought patterns to mature, healthy ones.

Whereas I'm pleased with the person I became and the man I ended up with, I wish I had gotten here via another path. I am sad to say, that I have found that the highly touted strategy of playing the field to prepare oneself for marital bliss is misleading and overrated. It's true that it does enable a person to refine likes and dislikes and personal criteria for a mate. And if we could just do that it would be okay. The collateral damage we don't hear about is how all those experiences pollute our mind and heart for years and decades – I can attest to that much anyway – and maybe even our entire life. Do you know what one love that ends in a broken heart, another love that ends in a hardened heart, and still another that results in a forever-longing heart add up to? A person with a broken, hardened and forever-longing heart. Is that what you want to bring into a relationship?

There is a better way, the way God would have led me, had I followed Him and not gone my own way. Although my dating experiences gave me valuable perspective, they also had some very undesirable consequences, one of which pertains to our proverb.

First of all, the white wedding dress wasn't fooling anyone as I walked down the isle with a six-year-old daughter. On my wedding day, I hoped I could put my prodigal years in the past and start anew with my heart completely dedicated to my husband. The problem is that the old cliché about putting the past behind you is just a cute play on words. In a spiritual sense, we can effectively turn our back on the past through the victory we claim in Christ. In a practical, physical sense, we still have to live with the natural consequences of our past.

I am completely committed to my husband, but I confess I cannot delete my memory. Consequently, the most mundane things unintentionally cause me to recall experiences with old boyfriends. For instance, long piers, great white sharks and the Spanish word for "hill" all remind me of a certain Italian surfer I once loved. Bagels and lox, the Zionist movement and Rosh Hashanah on the calendar remind me of a Jewish soldier I once loved. I dated so diversely and for so long, that there is very little in life that doesn't remind me of some past relationship, and often, they are fond memories. As soon as I become aware that I'm dwelling on the past, I shut the memories down and focus on the present again. However, at times, I can be consumed in those thoughts of the past for many minutes before I realize where my mind is. Does this sound conducive to a successful marriage?

My husband has consuming memories of his own, I'm sure. There's nothing we can do to erase those memories. However, we have a mutually agreed upon philosophy that, in general, we should not rehash old relationship stories with each other. I'm afraid I often forget myself and out will pop a quirky anecdote that involved a former boyfriend. Fortunately, my husband always reacts with some of those wonderful qualities for which I married him: patience, tolerance and understanding.

If I could redesign my past, I would have lived in a family with happily married parents, hit adulthood with a healthy criterion for selecting a life partner and yes, I still would have dated some, but I never would have allowed myself to fall in love with someone I knew I didn't have a future with. I would have kept my heart pure and given it only to one man. I would have kept my body pure and let my first sexual experience permanently bond me to my husband. This isn't some idealist fantasy; it's God's will for us. I know people who had just this experience and are very happily married. I admire those people.

Hold this thought: I will save not only my body, but also my heart for my husband.

It's a Biological Thang

For these commands are a lamp, this teaching is a light, and the corrections of discipline are the way to life, keeping you from the immoral man, from the smooth tongue of the wayward man. Do not lust in your heart after his good looks or let him captivate you with his eyes, for the gigolo reduces you to a loaf of bread, and the adulterer preys upon your very life. Can a person scoop fire into her lap and not get burned? Can a person walk on hot coals without her feet being scorched?

Proverbs 6:23-28

56

Women love dangerous men. Though not quite a fact of life, it's at least a general tendency. I believe there are women who have made only wise dating and marriage choices, but I think most young women at some point have been attracted to Mr. G. Q. Wrong. Sure, he's so fly and looks so fresh in his Abercrombie, but he's a player! And while we should be repulsed by the fact that he has a different woman as the seasons change, we secretly wish we could be one of them.

If we have a healthy self-respect, we may not fall into the player's trap. Our desire to live according to God's law and have a healthy relationship may enable us to understand that what we're looking for cannot be had with Mr. Wrong. However, if our souls are needy or our self-esteem weak, such a conquest may seem to be just what we need to feel better about ourselves. Being his girl will earn us respect. Being his girl will elevate us to a higher social level. And we may have a little bit of the co-dependent tendency to believe that *we* are the ones that can make the Mr. Wrongs of life change their gigolo ways and settle down.

I pray that we will listen to the words of this proverb and understand what so many women have found out through years of chasing the wrong type of men and the resulting heartache. Mr. G. Q. Wrong will reduce us to a piece of meat, or, as Solomon says, a loaf of bread. He will come along with a sweet, sultry song, lure us in, consume us and make a light snack of our self-esteem. Even if no one else ever finds out what happened between the two of us, the memory of how that man used us will torture us.

Maybe we think, "Two can play that game. I'll use him before he uses me." Okay. So now we're no better than he is.

Maybe we think, "That won't happen to me. I'll just date him long enough to add the trophy to my shelf and I won't let myself get attached to him." Are we the first women to have thought we could play with fire and not get burned? Our proverb says, "Can a person walk on hot coals without her feet being scorched?" Those words are over 3,000 years old! This is not a game we can win.

A woman's seemingly self-destructive attraction to the most cocky and best-looking man actually has a socio-biologically adaptive basis. Our physical bodies are unconsciously looking for the man who will produce the best offspring, though on a conscious level, we just think he looks hot. Recognizing that our strong attraction has a biological function may help us understand and overcome the tendency to be attracted to Mr. G. Q. Wrong. Just as with other biological tendencies we must overcome, such as that of natural defensiveness against people who look different than we do, we can rise above our physical bodies by using the magnificent mind that God gave us and calling on His spirit to fill our conscious thought.

For our own good – for

> Maybe we think, "Two can play that game. I'll use him before he uses me." Okay. So now we're no better than he is.

57

our heart's sake – we must make decisions about who to date based on a more sensible criterion than the "hot scale." Though we may think we have no control over who we find attractive, if we determine to do so, we will find we can cultivate an attraction to Mr. Right. The first step is to stop attending to Mr. G. Q. Wrong and look around for Mr. Right. He doesn't call attention to himself like G. Q. does. He's going about his business. He's studying; he's working; he may be on the same sports team as G. Q., but he is a team player and doesn't strut when he scores – which is probably why we never noticed him before. His name is not in the rumor mill because, well, he may never have been with a girl before.

With Mr. Right awaits the love that our heart desires. And as the days, weeks, months and years go by, his face, which at first we may have thought ordinary, will become preciously handsome to us. Then we will have it all – a man with good looks and a great personality. Isn't that what we're really looking for?

Hold this thought: I won't make my dating decisions based on looks.

The Helpful Green-Eyed Monster

Anger is cruel and fury overwhelming, but who can stand before jealousy?

Proverbs 27:4

Anger, fury, jealousy: Are these bad things? No.

God experiences all of these and God is 100 percent pure good, so it stands to reason that nothing that God experiences is bad. Having been made in God's image, we also experience the natural emotions of anger, fury and jealousy. And just as God does, we can experience these without sin. When these tempting emotions do result in sin, in our anger we become cruel, in our fury we're completely overwhelmed. And in our jealousy? Who can stand before jealousy turned sinful? Jealousy unchecked is the most destructive human emotion and it's capable of anything!

So we should try to avoid ever feeling jealous, right? We use an expression "jealousy rears its ugly head" or call jealousy "the green-eyed monster," but I believe that's a lie of Satan. Jealousy is a woman's friend. Just like our other emotions, jealousy is feedback from some of the parts of our being that we're not so carefully monitoring all the time. Jealousy is a red flag, a warning sign that something precious to us is pulling away from us or that someone (or something) else is encroaching on our precious relationship. We need to heed jealousy and take action that will bring that precious relationship back into balance.

Jealousy is a first sign of a relationship in jeopardy. It might be trying to tell us that we've been neglecting someone we love. Maybe the action we need to take is to reprioritize. Or maybe jealousy is trying to tell us that the person we love is losing focus and we need to intervene to make our loved one aware of this. Maybe jealousy is trying to tell us both things at once.

My husband started college when he was 37 years old. He went to a small, private school where there were not a lot of nontraditional students. He was the "old man" about campus. Of course, the thought occurred to me (almost daily) that he was surrounded by beautiful, young women. I quieted those thoughts with the assurance that he loves me, our marriage is very important to him and that he's mature enough not to be charmed by a 20-year old. (OK, that last part was probably self-delusional – he's a man, after all.)

During the three years it took him to get his degree, there were a few times I felt jealous. One semester, he kept telling stories around the dinner table about this one girl in particular. The first time or two, I didn't think anything about it, but when the dinnertime reports were coming in almost daily about this girl, it hit a nerve. At first, I just let those feelings run in the background and if anything, they made me a little angry toward him. I tried to ignore my feelings, but feelings won't be ignored. When we don't express the feelings we're having, they create other feelings we will express. My jealousy was coming out sideways as anger and that only served to perpetuate what was actually happening – that my husband was becoming less fascinated with me and more fascinated with some skinny blonde who drove a BMW.

When I finally got to the point of addressing the subject with my husband, I could not control my emotions. I very passionately told him he needed to nip his interest of this girl in the bud. His reaction: "What interest?" He honestly was taken aback to learn that I thought he had a thing for this girl. But he did have a thing for her; he just hadn't realized it until I brought it to his attention. His realization wasn't immediate. After a few days of reflection, he admitted that he had been dwelling on her inordinately. He was like the frog in the frying pan in this instance, not even realizing he was in danger.

Girls, here's something that's going to sound crazy, and trust me, I don't understand it myself, but many men can walk all the way down an errant path and get to the very end before they realize where they are. It could be that men are less self-aware than women. However, I believe it has to do with that mechanism of denial that we all possess. Many women use denial to continue on in relationships they know from early on to be abusive. Others use it to eat Twinkies to the point of obesity. Most of us have some weakness that we are capable of turning an internal blind eye to until it has completely consumed us. For many men, it's lust. I believe that a man can be completely unaware of (or in complete denial about) a danger until his pants are down around his ankles. 61

As women, we can reject this premise and hold our boyfriends or spouses fully responsible for themselves – and be devastated when they cheat on us – or we can heed the message of jealousy and intervene on their behalf, saving our relationships. Everybody who's lost in denial needs an intervention – a caring person to shake them up and make them see what's real and where they are headed. This is Biblical! Isaiah 58:1 (*The Message*) says, "Shout! A full-throated shout! Hold nothing back – a trumpet-blast shout! Tell my people what's wrong with their lives." We should do that for our loved ones. Shake them up and make them see. If with eyes wide open they decide they like the direction they are going, then we can hold them fully responsible.

Most of all, I prescribe this shake up for us, the women, as a healthy expression of jealousy. If we will do what jealousy is asking of us early on, it won't build up and send us over the edge with a force greater than anger and fury put together.

Hold this thought: I won't let jealousy build up inside me.

A Cinderella Story

Hope deferred makes a heart sick, but a longing fulfilled is a tree of life.

Proverbs 13:12

This is a simple observation with profound, compassionate insight. There's no advice here, yet it's wisdom all the same. What's to be done about dreams that won't come true? They are life's greatest frustrations and disappointments because we usually cannot do anything about them! We can't make someone love us. We can't conjure a wonderful spouse out of thin air. We can't bring people back to life.

I've had a lot of dreams that didn't come true, but with the passing of time and some reflection, I realized that what I had hoped would happen wasn't the best for me and that things turned out much better. This is God watching out for us – at times denying our requests in our best interest.

But once, I had a dream that didn't come true and time didn't make it better. The door was closed never to reopen and nothing could happen to make me feel like it was the best thing for me.

Night after night I sat thinking about my loss and how there was absolutely no way to reverse or change it. I thought I might go mad for the great yearning to have someone who under no circumstances I could have. The person I wanted was gone forever from this world. And no one can ever come along to take his place. Even if I do have another child, no one can ever take away the yearning for the one I lost.

My dream was to see my baby's blue eyes shining in the sun. I didn't get to. My heart is sick.

Despite the finality of death, I have hope that my longing will one day be fulfilled. Yes, even death does not have to end a dream. With a deliberate faith, I believe I will see my baby's blue eyes when I no longer measure time in minutes, hours and days. That is the thought I hold in front of me. Instead of thinking about the past – the heinous memory of the series of events that robbed me of my dream – I hold a thought from the future: A large hammock strung high up between two limbs of the tree of life where my baby and I can rock eternal days away as butterflies and hummingbirds flitter about us and a tangerine glow sets into amethyst mountain peaks. That's the vision I have. And though it is most definitely a deferred hope, keeping the dream of what I want in front of me – versus focusing on how I still don't have what I hoped for – keeps my thoughts positive and my sick heart hanging on.

63

I have always loved that song that Cinderella sings in the Disney classic movie as she's mopping the floor. Through my jaded youth I thought it was the stuff of fairy tales. Now I see her song as a statement of faith and a choice to remain hopeful. Remember the words?

> "A dream is a wish your heart makes when you're fast asleep. In dreams you will lose your heartache, whatever you wish for you'll keep. Have faith in your dreams and some day that rainbow will come shining through. No matter how your heart is grieving, if you keep on believing, the dream that you wish will come true."

Do you have a dream that hasn't come true yet? There are two ways we can think about our hopes and dreams. We can focus on the fact that we still don't have what we want or we can focus on the future when our longing will be fulfilled. Focusing on what

I thought I might go mad for the great yearning to have someone who under no circumstances I could have. The person I wanted was gone forever from this world.

we don't have only exaggerates our heartsickness and that's no way to live life.

"One thing I do, forgetting those things which are behind, I reach forward to the goal for the prize of the upward call of God in Christ Jesus" (Philippians 3:13-14).

Hold this thought: Every dream can have a happy ending – given enough time.

chapter three

Beauty Secrets from the Proverbs

There are Some Things
even Accessories Can't Hide

You Have Quite a Reputation

How to Gracefully Pick Yourself Up

Where Credit is Due

For Lips that Drip Honey, Try This!

You Are *How* You Eat

Conduct Becoming of a Lady

Chill Pill: Take One Daily or As Needed

Pet Peeves, Pests in Disguise

There are Some Things
even Accessories Can't Hide

Like a gold ring in a pig's snout is a beautiful woman who shows no discretion.

Proverbs 11:22

For a long time, when considering this proverb, I pictured a beautiful young woman who was loud and boisterous and scantily dressed. I thought the meaning of this verse was that all that beauty was wasted on a person who flaunts it so much that she makes it appear ridiculous. It would be like owning a fur coat and then wearing it everywhere you go – to ballgames, to the gym, to pump gas; it is taking a thing of beauty and making it appear worthless from overexposure.

Then I looked up the word "discretion" in the dictionary and discovered that whereas it could possibly be construed to address modest behavior, the true definition is "cautious behavior." A discreet person is one who weighs carefully what she says and does – a person who does not act rashly. An additional definition is being able to keep a secret when needed.

Back in Solomon's day, it was not uncommon for beautiful women to wear rings in their noses (and it didn't have the connotations of a ring in the nose today). Picture a beautifully adorned woman in fine, flowing, wispy silk robes with ornate dangling earrings and a gold ring in her nose. She's the fashion icon of the sixth century B.C. She causes chariot wrecks as she crosses the street!

Now Solomon knows her well, so she doesn't have the same effect on him. He says that in all this beauty, the only thing of redeeming value he sees is the gold ring in her nose. Aside from that ring, he sees only swine when he contemplates this woman because she has no discretion. She acts rashly; she does whatever occurs to her without considering the consequences. She acts on impulse, emotion and physical sensation. This, in Solomon's eyes, makes her no better than an animal – and not just any animal, but one that wallows in the mud.

And indeed, discretion is one of the things that separate us from the animals.

I have a dog that sleeps inside the house. He is good buddies with neighboring dogs that sleep outside. Quite often, something exciting (to a dog) will happen in the middle of the night, like an armadillo spotting, and the neighboring dogs outside will go crazy. This wakes my inside dog and, with absolutely no consideration whatsoever for the sleeping people in the house, he will start to bark and whimper and prance around to be let outside. *It's a hunt! I've got to go!* He gives no thought to who he is impacting with his impulsiveness.

A person, on the other hand, is endowed with the ability to apply abstract thought to a situation and think beyond what she feels and wants. She is able to consider how what she wants and intends to do will impact others. We *have* the ability. But, we must opt to *engage* this ability.

A discreet woman has her abstract cognition switch always in the "engaged" position. A discreet woman, even in chaotic and rushed circumstances, can quickly go through the mental exercise of imagining how what she says and does will impact other people. And a discreet and wise woman will choose to say and do those things that ultimately will have a positive impact on other people.

Regardless of what you're wearing, that's true beauty.

Hold this thought: Outer beauty is no good without inner beauty.

67

You Have Quite a Reputation

*A good name is more desirable than great riches; to be esteemed is
better than silver or gold.*

Proverbs 22:1

In the late teen years, we become acutely aware of and probably begin to resent stereotypes. We see how unfair it is for the
person who loves to dress in black to be labeled "Goth" when
we know this person to actually be a fun-loving "goof," and for
the sporty girl with short hair to be labeled "dyke" when we
know she's had a crush on the same guy since third grade. Stereotypes are bunk! We can resist them all we want, vow never
to hold any ourselves, but we can't make them go away.

Humans are hard-wired to quickly categorize others; it's a
survival mechanism that was needed much more in the first
95 percent of human history than it is today. Today, we largely
need to overcome our propensity to classify people in order
to not just survive but thrive in this world. Good for you if you
make the concerted effort on a daily basis to resist seeing people first as rednecks, New Yorkers, jocks, cheerleaders, punks,
emos, lowriders, sluts, posers, Nazis, Asians, anorexics, dorks
and all the other labels we can put on people based on their
appearance or brief observations of their behavior.

However, just because we reject stereotypes, doesn't mean
they reject us. They cling to us all and that's an unjust matter of
fact. Not caring what others think of us won't keep them from
thinking about us. Likewise, although we may not care what
they think, they do, and how they treat us, in part, is going to
be based on the categories they have put us in with the little
information we provide them on first meeting, at church on
Sunday morning, as we cut them off in traffic, pass them in the
hall, etc.

We're not immune from stereotypes even when we get to know people better. Last Sunday at 11:59 a.m., just as the pastor was making his closing appeal, my cell phone rang and … I didn't have my ringer off. I hadn't been as embarrassed as I was in those 10 swollen seconds since … the last time my phone rang in church. Yep, that makes two times for me in a matter of a couple of months. When I got up to leave, a young lady came up to me and said, "You're getting a reputation."

Wow. Just two cell phone goofs in two months creates a reputation? It's not like I'm intentionally being rude – I just forget to turn the phone off. That doesn't seem that unusual to me, but in this particular congregation it is. In fact, I don't remember anyone else's phone ever ringing in church. So now I've got a rep of either being a rude cell phone user or Alzheimic. That's probably not going to ruin my run for presidency but do you see how easy it is to get a reputation? It literally only takes doing something twice to earn one.

I've been going to the same church for over three years. The young lady who told me I'm getting a rep knows me well and knows I'm neither a rude cell phone user nor Alzheimic. No matter – my behavior, however uncharacteristic, provided her with information she needed to sort and store me in a neat category. So I'm filed in her mind under "Donna/cell phone habits/

Good for you if you make the concerted effort on a daily basis to resist seeing people as rednecks, New Yorkers, jocks, cheerleaders, punks, emos, lowriders, sluts, posers, Nazis, Asians, anorexics, dorks and all the other labels we can put on people based on their appearance or brief observations of their behavior.

rude" or "Donna/memory/poor."

I don't deserve that note in her files, but there is something in her files that I do deserve: "Donna/congenitally, chronically tardy."

Yes, I have a bad habit of being late and it seems to be a genetic thing. In general, I arrive either right on time or a few minutes late. Either way, it drives my husband nuts because he's the type who thinks being on time is being 10 minutes early.

One Sunday when my church was honoring recent graduates from high school and college, my husband was to be among them because he was graduating with a teaching degree. In our typical fashion, we arrived a few minutes late and because of it, my husband missed the presentation to the graduates with which they had opened the service. Being late never bothers me too much, but that day it did very much. I felt very small for causing him to miss a well-deserved moment of recognition.

On the way home that morning, my husband said in all sincerity, "They should have known better than to put something involving the Schillingers first in the order of service." Ouch.

Sometimes the things we do to warrant a bad rep come back to bite us in an obvious way. More often, we probably miss opportunities we didn't even know existed because of our bad reps. For instance, I doubt anyone would ever ask me to lead the worship service because of my reputation of being chronically tardy. Maybe I have been considered for such a responsibility before and dismissed as not being suitable because of my "condition." Maybe someone who knows about my condition has before been in the position to recommend me for a job but has taken that little piece of information they know about me and applied it to my work ethic and responsibility in general and deemed me "unreliable." That may be unfair and inaccurate, but it's not unfounded. Their erroneous generalizations are based in fact – my irresponsible chronic tardiness.

I can honestly say, "I don't care what people think of me

coming in one or two minutes late to a meeting or a service." But I cannot say, "I don't care if my chronic tardiness results in lost jobs and other opportunities," because I do care. As much as I think they should be able to, people can't isolate that one behavior of mine and not let it impact any of their other thoughts or impressions about me.

My tardiness and indeed all my and your actions are like pebbles thrown in the pond, causing a ripple and reverberating far beyond our ability to keep track of them. The same is true of our positive actions. If we care about friends, happiness, success or love, we have to care what people think of us – how we dress, the words we use, how we act, how we drive and what we do when we get mad. It's all fodder for the reputation that is developing around us whether we give a rip or not.

Hold this thought: If I have to have a rep, I want a good one.

How to Gracefully Pick Yourself Up

When pride comes, then comes disgrace, but with humility comes wisdom.

Proverbs 11:2

Pride goes before destruction, a haughty spirit before a fall.

Proverbs 16:18

72

A woman's pride brings her low, but a woman of lowly spirit gains honor.

Proverbs 29:23

Everyone has had an experience of pride followed by a fall – some quite literally, like the person who finishes a triumphant speech to roaring rounds of applause only to trip as she's leaving the podium. It's only natural to feel elated and happy with ourselves when we've just had a success. And for people with a lot of natural abilities, this feeling comes quite often. A naturally talented or beautiful person may have a real problem with pride.

I am a very intelligent person – and that's not pride talking, it's a simple fact. I also "pride myself" on being a frugal and shrewd person who is not fooled by marketing gimmicks. I often receive emails about special promotions such as, "Try our service free for one month with no obligation to continue and get a $20 gift card – free!" To me, that is easy pickins'. These gimmicks rely not so much on people liking the service or product as they do on people forgetting they signed up for it and being too disorganized to cancel before their trial period is over. But I mark my calendar with the phone number to call to cancel on the last business day of my free trial and I end up owing nothing and getting free stuff and services. I've got those gimmicks beat! Or so I proudly thought.

One such offer I got was for some lip repair product – supposed to make lips look plumper and wrinkles disappear. The deal was: Try the product free for 30 days and if I liked it, the company would send me shipments of the product every 60 days. The product was really expensive – about $60 for 3 tiny vials of something that, in my opinion, was about as effective as Chapstick. Before my 30 days were out, I called to cancel and that was that.

As I used the hyped-up lip gloss every day I would shake my head in dismay thinking, "I can't believe some poor fool would actually pay $60 for this stuff." A few weeks later, I got my credit card statement and found out that I was that poor fool. I called the company and they explained to me, and I later confirmed by checking my original e-mail offer, that I could use the product for free for 30 days, and if I didn't want to continue receiving it and I didn't want to be charged for the trial, I had to return the unused portion in the original box before the 30 days was up. Now every day as I use the product I say to myself, "I can't believe that I'm the poor fool who actually paid $60 for this stuff." I'm so embarrassed about it, I never told my husband (but I guess he knows now).

Our natural and cultivated abilities and gifts do not make us foolproof. Even a beauty queen can go around all day with spinach stuck in her teeth. And oh, the humiliation when we realize how false was our pride. These humiliating moments have real staying power in the memory too, which is good. For it's usually when the last humiliating memory fades that we're due to create a new one.

I Corinthians 4:9 (LB) says, "What are you so puffed up about? What do you have that God hasn't given you? And if all you have is from God, why act as though you are so great, and as though you have accomplished something on your own?"

The talents and abilities in which we take pride are natural gifts that we've had since birth. Yes, we may have cultivated them, but even the ability to do that is because of God's grace. If we stand tall with beautiful features, if we are creative, good problem-solvers, good communicators or have sound judgment, it is because God allows it.

What if one day God no longer allows it? Can our destiny change in one day? Sure, it can. One day a talented, handsome, intelligent actor, Christopher Reeves, was riding his horse, something he was very good at. His horse didn't quite make a jump and the actor was hurled to the ground head first. The injuries to his neck paralyzed him for life. From that day forward, he never walked on his own again, he never went to the bathroom or brushed his teeth or even ate on his own again. And his once good looks were gone, too. His life took on new meaning as he began to advocate for research that could provide a cure for his situation and that of others with similar disabilities. Life was certainly not over, but all those gifts and talents in which a person usually takes pride – all but intelligence – were gone or practically useless. The man who made his mark in cinema by portraying Superman ended life as weak as a Superman in the presence of kryptonite – he died of an infection caused by a bedsore.

I'm not saying Christopher Reeves' fall was a result of pride. Only God knows why his life ran the course it did. One thing I can say for certain about Reeves' life, however, is that God used him in his humbled state. Indeed, in his lowly spirit, he gained honor.

When we've fallen flat in a big way or even a small way, let God lift us up and set our

> Our natural and cultivated abilities and gifts do not make us foolproof. Even a beauty queen can go around all day with spinach stuck in her teeth.

feet back on God's path. Knowing we have a positive personal relationship with the Creator of the universe – that we can call the Creator "Father" – is a never-failing source of self-esteem that will elate and elevate us in a lasting way that false pride can't touch. The self-esteem that comes from being a child of God is stable and permanent. In contrast, pride in ourselves has no staying power – it is always followed by a fall.

Hold this thought: All my abilities are gifts from God.

Where Credit is Due

Before her downfall, a woman's heart is proud, but humility comes before honor.

Proverbs 18:12

"Abhor" is a strong word – I think even stronger than "hate," though it's synonymous. And that is how God feels about us taking credit for things He does.

Do you know why God loved Moses so much – why God allowed Moses to be in His presence several times during his life? It's because Moses was humble – the Bible says he was the most humble man on earth (Numbers 12:3). Yet by human standards, he had more reason than anyone on earth to be proud. Though he was born into slavery, he was raised in the court of one of the most powerful rulers of his time – raised like his son. Later, when that went sour, he upgraded to direct communication with the Creator of the universe. Then, with some minor help of a spokesman, he freed an entire ethnic group from slavery and led them to safety. He spoke the word and the Red Sea parted! If I were able to part the waters of even a seasonal creek, I'd feel pretty darn special. But not Moses. The more human reasons he had to feel pride, the more humility he felt because he recognized that none of these accomplishments were his own. The fact that he took no pride in the accomplishments but instead feared God even more at each success is what endeared him to God.

Why does God so despise pride? We can probably relate if we'll think about a time when we worked really hard to make something a success, despite the attitudes, objections and obstacles of those around us (maybe even people who are supposed to be helping us). Then when the effort succeeded, the person who least supported the idea and project all the

76

way through piped up to receive part of the glory. If this hasn't happened to you, it will, and maybe God allows us all that experience once so we can know a tiny bit of what it's like to be God – always having some upstart take the credit for what God has done.

Sometimes we need to be reminded just who is enabling every single thing we do all day long. I got a good reminder a couple of weeks ago while sitting in my truck. I changed positions and as I did, something slipped in my lower back and as far as I can discern, my femoral nerve, the one that runs from my lower back through my pelvis and down the front of my leg, was pinched. That nerve might be as big around as a piece of yarn – it's certainly no major body organ – but when it was tweaked it brought me to my knees, literally. The pain disabled me for days. Just like when you cut your pinky finger, you suddenly realize how much you actually use that little appendage, that tweaked nerve made me appreciate my overall good health and the One who grants it to me each day, enabling me to be me!

I was also struck by the fact that I didn't do anything foolish to incur that injury. It's not like I was skydiving or even skiing. I was literally sitting reading a book in a parked vehicle. How much safer can you get? Health and well-being are daily gifts from God. God gives them and God can take them away even without any help from us.

When we finally comprehend our complete dependence on God and come to the point where we won't steal the credit, God can do great things through us. It will be clear that our good deeds and great accomplishments are God's power at work in us. Through our success people will want to know God – they'll want to know what fuels us!

It's impractical if not impossible to acknowledge God's power at all times. If there were one word that meant, "Thank God for enabling me to do it," we'd have to say it 1,000 times a day, and that might only begin to express the truth of the matter. It is practical, however, and highly recommended, that we start and end each day with a moment to reflect on how God is enabling our life, health, intelligence, opportunity, love, security – all the things we take for granted – as well as those extraordinary blessings.

I often pray, "Thank you, Father, for allowing me to be a woman in the 21st century in the United States." What incredible advantage I have in life by virtue of when and where I was born! That's just the beginning of the innumerable factors completely out of my control by which God's blessing makes me who I am.

Hold this thought: God deserves the credit for every good thing.

For Lips that Drip Honey, Try This!

An anxious heart weighs a person down, but a kind word cheers her up.

Proverbs 12:25

The tongue that brings healing is a tree of life…

Proverbs 15:4a

Pleasant words are a honeycomb, sweet to the soul and healing to the bones.

Proverbs 16:24

Try this: The next time you have a personal conversation with friends, coworkers or family, listen to everything that comes out of your mouth for about 10 minutes. It's hard! As soon as you pay attention to what you're saying, you can't help but censor yourself. But try to just be a listener without interfering with what you're saying.

What did you notice? Were your words negative, neutral or positive?

Often when I catch myself listening in on my own conversations, I'm a little embarrassed at what a whiner I can be! Where does all that negativity come from?

The media sets a negative societal tone, for one. Our modern ability to comb the world for news results in endless fodder for negativity. If we can't find tragedy or something bizarre to complain about in our own back yard, the media will import some bad news from another country. Nonetheless, we can't blame the media because, after all, it's just a social institution made up of people.

People have probably always liked to talk more about what's wrong than what's right. It's normal. But why be normal if normal means negative? Here's a great place to channel some of that youthful nonconformist energy. Despite constant negativity around us, we can choose to be positive people. The proverbs above remind us why it's important. Being positive cheers and brings healing to body and soul; it's intangible honey. And do you know who is the most likely to benefit from all that verbal honey? We are!

Our own kind words will cheer *us* up. Our own pleasant words will keep *us* physically and emotionally healthy – yes, they can even heal bones, as our scripture says!

The July 2006 *Journal of American Academy of Orthopaedic Surgeons* reported a study that concluded, "Refraining from worry, anxiety and other negative moods and adopting a positive attitude are paramount to an orthopaedic patient's physical surgery outcome and recovery speed." Patricia H. Rosenberger, Ph.D., associate research scientist in the Department of Epidemiology and Public Health at Yale University School of Medicine, and lead author of the article, said, "Psychosocial factors play a large role in a patient's physical surgical outcomes, not just their quality of life."

Solomon knew centuries ago what scientists are now substantiating through objective research. How apt that bone doctors have rediscovered this ancient truth. If pleasant words can speed the healing of a broken bone, think what they can do for you today!

Now try this: the next time you have a personal conversation with friends, coworkers or family, focus on what you're saying and try to make it positive.

Hold this thought: Be different. Be positive.

80

You Are *How* You Eat

She who loves pleasure will become poor; whoever loves wine and oil will never be rich.

Proverbs 21:17

In the house of the wise are stores of choice food and oil, but a foolish woman devours all she has.

Proverbs 21:20

Do not join those who drink too much wine or gorge themselves on meat, for drunkards and gluttons become poor and drowsiness clothes them in rags.

Proverbs 23:20-21

"When I was your age, I could eat whatever I wanted and not gain weight." Sound familiar? I know I've said that to my daughter a time or two and it is true. Young women burn calories quicker than older women do. Starting at about age 18, a woman's metabolism starts to slow down and it grinds to just above a standstill by the time she hits 60.

When I was young, not only could I eat anything I wanted, I did. And with no restraint on my food choices, I developed a keen sweet tooth. I consider myself an expert on pies – from key lime to pecan. And fudge and truffles and pastry and on and on. Though those dessert days were memorable, I wish someone had instructed me and guided me to get into the habit of eating correctly when I was young. Instead, with that same "eat for the moment" mentality, I went off to college on a three-times a day, all-you-can-eat meal plan. The result – the freshman 15 – 15 pounds gained in my freshman year. It was probably the ice cream bar that did it.

Actually, whether it be all-you-can-eat or hardly anything to eat, most women will gain weight beginning at age 18. It's how we go from a girlish figure to a woman's figure and it happens whether we go to college or right into the work world or get married and start having babies. It's a fact of life – the older we get, the slower our metabolism and thus, we gain weight.

Some women learn to compensate for this metabolic slow-down more quickly and easily than others. Those women are self-disciplined. They can make themselves exercise when they don't feel like it. Even when surrounded by wedding cake and punch, boxes of Krispy Kremes or a dessert bar at Golden Corral, they limit themselves to a small portion – if they take any at all!

Do you think they don't enjoy ice cream as much as the rest of us? I think these highly disciplined women do love the taste of food just as much as the rest of us. I think the difference in them and well, me, is that their rational, realistic thinking remains engaged even when they're passing the dessert bar. And after years and years of reminders that late night pizza or pecan pie will go straight to their thighs, they have finally internalized it to the point that they no longer have to give the matter any conscious thought – sensible eating is a habit and way of life.

I know that there are a variety of physical conditions that can result in a person being overweight, and right now I'm not talking about people who have one of those. But for the rest of us, our problem is that we don't resist the things that tempt us – the sweets, pasta, bread, fried foods and junk food. And on the flip side, we don't exercise sufficiently to work off the calories in excess of what our bodies need as essential fuel.

Why? Because we lack discipline. Don't hate me for saying that. I don't like to browbeat – and I'm making a confession about myself here, as well. For several years now I have been trying and trying to drop 30 pounds. I put it on at a stressful time in my life, about seven years ago, and have not been able to get it off since. I can blame the stress for having gained the weight, but that is not really the root cause. Fit people live under a great deal of stress too. The root cause is that from girl-hood up, I never learned to control my eating.

My father was a binge/purge eater. He would go day after day with no breakfast and very little lunch and then when we went out to eat on Sunday after church, he would really pack it in – including finishing whatever was left on the kids' plates. He would revel in his feasting. Watching him pack it away actually made for some good childhood memories. In fact, one of my favorite memories of my father is when he had taken me to work with him one day (I was about 14) and we had worked the morning and into the early afternoon without eating and we were ravenous. He took me to a pie factory, a place where they baked the pies for many area restaurants, and we bought a co-conut cream pie. We sat down opposite each other at the one booth in the wholesale pie place and dug into that pie. About two-thirds of the way through the pie, we sat back, looked at each other and groaned. Ah, good times! And yet, the sad real-ity is that we had each just consumed about a day's worth of calories – mostly made up of sugar and fat.

There are a lot of things in life that we can legitimately credit or blame our parents for; our eating patterns are one of them. However, just like all those other things, both good and bad, that we picked up from our parents, when we're on our own, we have a choice to keep them or toss them out. It's a lot easier to keep them than to shed 18 years of behavioral conditioning. However,

I think these highly disciplined women do love the taste of food just as much as the rest of us. I think the difference in them and well, me, is that their rational, realistic thinking remains engaged even when they're passing the dessert bar.

if we've inherited a poor self-discipline when it comes to eating and exercise, we must make the effort to change! Even if we are not overweight now, we should start to change our unhealthy patterns, because they will catch up with us! I was in my mid-30s before my gluttonous sweet tooth caught up with me. If you think reversing 18 years is hard, try changing 35 years of behavioral conditioning!

I read the results of a seemingly silly little study some social scientist conducted once to prove a point about change. And boy, does it ever! Researchers asked their subjects, people who worked at a desk with a garbage can on one side, to move their garbage can to the other side. Then they tallied how many times it took people to begin to automatically go to the side where the garbage can was to throw something away. For an average of 57 times, people turned toward the wrong side, the old side where the can used to be, to try to throw away their garbage. The point is that if something as simple as learning to toss a wad of paper to the left when you're used to tossing to the right takes 57 tries before you get the hang of it, consider the effort and repetition needed to change eating habits of 18 years. (This is crazy, but after having read that study, I have made a point of periodically moving my trash can from place to place. Just when I feel like I'm nice and comfortable with one spot – bam! – I move it. I call it malleability conditioning.)

I wish my mom and dad had worked harder at developing my good eating and exercise habits. I wish they had modeled better habits. I can't dwell there though. I'm an adult now and I have my own choices to make. One of them is determining to do better by my own children and expose them to healthy foods, making eating good foods a family habit and helping them find a form of exercise that they will rely on to stay fit throughout life. Another choice is to improve my own habits for me, but also, again, for my kids, because what they see me doing will make much more of an impression on them than what they hear me saying.

I have focused almost exclusively on the health and fitness benefits of self-discipline in eating and exercise. But note now how our verses relate eating (and exercise) habits to prosperity. Solomon ties eating habits and income together with the common chord of self-discipline.

It would be oversimplifying things to say I'm overweight because I'm a lazy glutton, and even if there is some truth in that, it won't do me any good to dwell on it. Instead, I should focus on increasing self-discipline – the result of which will reflect favorably in everything from my waistline to my bank account.

85

Hold this thought: I will begin developing a good habit today.

Conduct Becoming of a Lady

Put away perversity from your mouth; keep corrupt talk far from your lips.

Proverbs 4:24

In this day and age, women can say anything – nothing is taboo. But does that mean we should say whatever we want?

It has been almost 100 years since women stepped up beside men in the public sphere of Western Civilization, but this relatively short amount of time, historically speaking, has not been sufficient for women to settle into their new identity as equals to men. Many women are enjoying the novelty of equality the way a 16-year-old boy hot rods around town when he first gets his driver's license. Some women revel in freedoms that were formerly prohibited, from sexual expression to smoking cigars, as if they were playing with new toys. Even the young women of today, who never suffered gross inequalities, boldly experiment with equalities just because they can.

When women truly settle into their new identity as social and intellectual equals to men, I believe that we will see a maturing of feminist behavior. As a group, women will begin to evaluate the benefit and efficacy of certain freedoms that are available to us. Yes, we have the ability and liberty to do, say and be whatever we want, but does this mean that it is to our benefit to do so? Is everything within our reach worth grabbing?

Some years ago, I read a *Newsweek* article about a teen girls' soccer team that was posed for a national championship. The reporter conducted part of the interview in the team's locker room where he noted the ambiance was remarkably similar to that of any boys' locker room, or for that matter, any men's rugby team locker room. The players were slapping each other around in horseplay, spitting on the floor and cursing like sailors.

Obviously, some women think that the pinnacle of women's liberation is the ability to behave in such a way that a bystander cannot distinguish on behavior alone a group of women from a group of men. This has led us to emulate not only upstanding men, but the worst kind of men, as well. I believe a mature view of women's liberation is acknowledging the ability to behave however we want and choosing to behave in ways that edify our collective identity and command respect from all – both men and women.

Fortunately, there are some standards of respectful behavior that have always applied equally to men and women. Though 100 years ago women may have been forbidden to curse, cursing has always been disreputable behavior in formal situations, such as at church or in front of a judge. Though 100 years ago it was unladylike for a woman to spit, spitting by man or woman alike has never been appropriate in certain places, such as inside a nice home or office building. Men have never been *carte blanche* socially banned from cursing, spitting or talking graphically about their love lives, like women were in the past; nonetheless there has always been a contingent of reputable men who restrain themselves from these oral perversities out of respect for themselves and others. Let these men be our equals. Women should also use self-restraint out of self-respect.

Thank God we live in a time in which women truly have freedom of speech, not just constitutionally, but socially. We can say whatever we want – no words are taboo. And yet, the words we choose to speak will define and distinguish us in one way or another. Whether we like it or not, or think it's fair or not, people form impressions of us based on what we say – this is true for guys too. This can be a good thing. We can use our words to stand out or to fit in.

I challenge you to distinguish yourself – stand out among your peers – by being the person they never heard curse or say

anything sexually graphic. You don't have to shoot stern looks
to others should they curse, just refrain from doing so yourself.
Of you, they will say with respect and almost disbelief, "I have
never heard her say a curse word."

As for fitting in – find some other way – like joining a community or intramural softball team or a choir.

*Hold this thought: I will distinguish myself by refraining from using
vulgar language.*

Chill Pill: Take One Daily or As Needed

A patient woman has great understanding, but a quick-tempered woman displays folly.

Proverbs 14:29

A hot-tempered woman stirs up dissension, but a patient woman calms a quarrel.

Proverbs 15:18

A fool gives full vent to her anger, but a wise woman keeps herself under control.

Proverbs 29:11

There's a scene in the movie "Friends with Money" that well echoes and illustrates the point about temper made in the first verse above. A woman is in an Old Navy store waiting in a long line to be checked out when a new register opens and the cashier calls, "I can take someone over here." So the woman proceeds to the empty check-out stand and, just short of arriving, a couple walks in from the side, cuts in front of her and hands their merchandise directly to the cashier. This makes the woman very angry. She's having a bad day anyway and this ices the cake. At first, she calmly points out to both cashier and couple what has happened – nobody cares. So her voice grows a little louder and she begins to insist the injustice be made right and still nobody cares. When she gets too loud to ignore, the cashier and couple try to quiet her, but still do not acknowledge that she was wronged, let alone do anything about it. She starts to lose it just as the manager comes along, and not knowing what has taken place, he only sees a woman who is losing control and he asks her to leave. This fuels the woman's fire and she goes nuts. The manager takes her by the arm; she struggles to get loose, makes a quick turn to leave the store on her own and mistakes a clear window for an open door. She walks smack into glass, bounces off and falls to the ground – blood everywhere. She's broken her nose.

Up until the part about being escorted out of the store, that scene is probably something everyone can relate to. Little injustices like losing our parking space, getting cut off in traffic and being cut in front of in line are common and they do bug! The great truth of this movie scene is that it doesn't matter how right we are, if we abandon rational behavior to try to prove our point, people won't believe us. We end up looking crazed and no one will listen to us. Clearly, no one was listening to this woman when she acted civilly either, and that also happens a lot. Being right doesn't matter as much as we were taught it would in grade school.

Whether it's a large or small injustice, a blatant insult or a frustration as simple as a traffic jam, remaining patient is always wise. "Patient" does not mean "not concerned." It does mean "in control." To lose control is to disgrace ourselves. If it happens in the presence of people we have to continue to interact with, like co-workers or peers, we've marked ourselves indelibly. We see high drama on television and in the movies all the time, but in real life, big acting does not win awards. One loss of control could cost us a promotion or our very job, a budding friendship or even a well-established one.

If in the fire of adversity, we keep our calm and maintain self-control – despite the burning inside – we will be throwing a wet blanket on the fire instead of feeding it. The proverb says a patient woman can calm a quarrel. It's interesting to note that

> We see high drama on television and in the movies all the time, but in real life, big acting does not win awards.

the verse does not say we can avoid a quarrel altogether. Life has inherent friction and even we "wise" women will be rubbed the wrong way. It's our reaction to the friction that counts.

I've heard many Christians speak against anger as if it is a sin. The Bible clearly does not convey this, particularly in the Old Testament where our very God was angry a lot! Anger is a perfectly natural reaction to injustice and frustrating circumstances, although James does say we should be "slow to become angry" (James 1:19). If our goal is to never grow angry, we will find ourselves failing time and time again. Instead, as Paul said, "In your anger, do not sin..." (Ephesians 4:26). Let's set a goal of remaining in control.

91

Hold this thought: I will stay cool in heated situations.

Pet Peeves, Pests in Disguise

Better a meal of vegetables where there is love than a fattened calf with hatred.

Proverbs 15:17

Better a dry crust with peace and quiet than a house full of feasting with strife.

Proverbs 17:1

92   *Better to live in a desert than with a quarrelsome and ill-tempered wife.*

Proverbs 21:19

Better to live on a corner of the roof than share a house with a quarrelsome wife.

Proverbs 25:24

When I was 10 years old, I got a green marker and recorded in my baby book a plan for my life: Marry Donald Corely at age 19, live in a big house and have four children. The world has changed a lot since I was 10, but for better or worse, 10-year-old girls still want to marry a popular guy, live in a big house and have kids (or at least pets!).

Domestic bliss is what we dream of from an early age – and that's OK, though I believe we should explore other dreams as well. When we look around and see how many people are married and have kids, that dream seems more like a foregone conclusion. Then look again and see how many marriages fail – one-half of them – and how the dream turns to a nightmare for the children caught in a divorce. What about the marriages that don't fail – some of those are nightmares too! Domestic bliss is indeed more dreamlike than we realize.

Why do so many marriages fail and why are so many others miserable? The answer is complex, but clearly some marriages suffer from an overcritical spouse – I know mine does and that spouse is me!

Thus far in my marriage, the average has been one big conflict a year that will take a few days if not weeks to work through. That's it, just one blow-out a year and those are usually met by both of us with even temperament and genuine concern to quickly resolve the problem.

The rest of the year my husband and I could be at peace – if I would allow it. I'm somewhat of a perfectionist and I like to keep a clean and organized house. I like the bathroom sinks to be continually hair- and muck-free. I like to have a full set of silverware. I like the scissors to stay in the same place. I expect people to wipe their feet on the doormat. I like the stovetop to be wiped down each day. If a dish says, "not dishwasher safe," I don't expect to see it in the dishwasher. I have nice towels that are not to be used for wiping off the dog when he comes in the house covered in mud. And the list goes on. Believe me, I could fill a few more pages with all the things I've been "training" my husband to do and not do.

My husband is a typical man and most men don't get the concept of "nice towels" or "not dishwasher safe," or even the doormat. It may be how they were raised and perhaps, with training, they could learn these concepts; or it may just be that a man's normal genetic make-up renders him oblivious to domestic details like keeping track of teaspoons.

Whatever the cause, is griping at him the solution? Sometimes my husband takes chide in stride and lets it roll off him like water off a duck's back. Other times, when he's tired or we were having a nice evening just before I started griping, I can see that my criticisms deflate him. He gets this aura that projects, "I can't do anything right for this woman."

93

That's not true. He's a kind, faithful spouse, he cares about my emotional and physical needs, he's a wonderful father, a hard worker and has no addictions! If I were to stack all of that on one side of a scale and on the other, all of his peccadilloes – losing flatware, tracking up the carpet, melting plastic containers in the dishwasher – how would the scale tip? Those important things he does well, though perhaps fewer in number, each weigh as much as a thousand peccadilloes. The scales don't lie: He's phat!

94   Can't I gladly pick up socks off the floor in exchange for a hard-working husband? Can't I put the toilet lid down in love for the loving father of my children? When I focus on the little irksome things on the lighter side of the scale, I'm adding weight to the undesirable side of my own scales. Yes, I've got scales too and though on the one side sit the heavy weights of "good mother" and "faithful," by adding enough griping and criticism to the other side, it is quite possible to tip the scales out of my favor to the extent that my husband might prefer to live alone than with cantankerous old me.

A clean house isn't worth my domestic bliss. I can go buy more towels and silverware, but this husband of mine was a gift from God. How could I replace him?

You know what? I didn't just become a nit-picky person after the honeymoon was over. I have been working on that one for many years before we even started dating!

Starting now, prepare yourself to let the little things go. Start becoming a person without pet peeves – a person who is not bothered by imperfection. You may have a lot of years of negative programming to reverse – I know I did.

Hold this thought: I will overlook the little things.

chapter four

Living La Vida Buena

Lotto – You Have to Play to Lose

Early to Rise, Still Wise

Start a Moss Collection Today   95

Laptop Envy

The Boob Tube

For a Real Eye-Opener, Count Sheep

Love Your Co-Signer as Yourself

I Want it All…Eventually

Lotto – You Have to Play to Lose

Lazy hands make a woman poor, but diligent hands bring wealth.
She who gathers crops in summer is a wise daughter, but she who sleeps during harvest is a disgraceful daughter.

Proverbs 10:4-5

She who works her land will have abundant food, but she who chases fantasies lacks judgment.

Proverbs 12:11

Diligent hands will rule, but laziness ends in slave labor.

Proverbs 12:24

Dishonest money dwindles away, but she who gathers money little by little makes it grow.

Proverbs 13:11

She who works her land will have abundant food, but the one who chases fantasies will have her fill of poverty.

Proverbs 28:19

When I was young, money was always a concern for my family. At times we lived below the poverty level and could have qualified for welfare. As I see it now with an adult perspective, our poverty reflected some of the principles discussed in these verses – mainly chasing fantasy and failure to gather money little by little.

I didn't learn how to get out of poverty when I was growing up; I didn't know the principles in these Proverbs – diligent work, capitalizing on your current resources and saving money. Instead, I spent a good amount of time daydreaming about ways to quickly change my status – everything from marry a rich man to win big on a game show to win the lottery. These are probably normal imaginings of a poor child.

Thank God I never had the sufficient desperation, motivation or chutzpah to follow through on most of my schemes – except the lottery tickets. Instead, as soon as I turned legal working age, I was out looking for a job. Even as the steady pay checks began to roll in from jobs in high school and college, the get-rich-quick schemes still swarmed around in my brain. I'll never know how much more successful I could have been in school and at saving money if I had abandoned that foolishness early on and applied to my life wise principles for acquiring wealth. It's not that I was always chasing leprechauns or anything, it's just that for a mind full of fantasies about hitting the jackpot, I lacked realistic focus.

97

Sometime in my 20s, it occurred to me that it is not my destiny to get rich quick. I surveyed my life and noted that for all the raffles, lotteries, gambling and seemingly easy-to-profit-from projects on which I'd wasted my time and money, none of them ever paid. I had never won more than $4 off a lottery ticket and had *never* won a raffle or even a door prize. When it came to winning, I was a big loser!

However, through a strong work ethic and God opening doors, I had managed to move up in position with each job change and was making more money at age 27 than my 50-year old mother was. That realization got my attention. I began to harness those fantasies about getting rich quick and redirect them to work on ways to use the resources I had currently

> Thank God I never had the desperation, motivation or chutzpah to follow through on most of my schemes – except the lottery tickets.

available to me to make more money.

Now my plans would take longer than one good day on "The Price is Right." It would take some years to complete graduate school and years of learning and practical experience to finally reach the position of executive director of a small organization when I was 31. Instead of the grand palace I used to fantasize about living in, I bought an investment cottage that I could barely afford and put a lot of elbow grease into fixing it up. When I sold my cherished cottage two and a half years later, I made a handsome profit – about as much as I could have won in the Showcase Showdown.

That might sound like success, but it was actually just like finishing a basic course – Money Management 101. I'm in an intermediate course now and still learning almost daily lessons about how to work diligently with the resources I presently have while saving money little by little. This is God's plan for our prosperity.

Hold this thought: I will work hard, use what I already have and save little by little.

Early to Rise, Still Wise

Go to the ant, you sluggard; consider its ways and be wise! It has no commander, no overseer or ruler, yet it stores its provisions in summer and gathers its food at harvest. How long will you lie there, you sluggard? When will you get up from your sleep? A little sleep, a little slumber, a little folding of the hands to rest – and poverty will come on you like a bandit and scarcity like an armed man.

Proverbs 6:6-11

I went past the field of the sluggard, past the vineyard of the woman who lacks judgment; thorns had come up everywhere, and the ground was covered with weeds, and the stone wall was in ruins. I applied my heart to what I observed and learned a lesson from what I saw; a little sleep, a little slumber, a little folding of the hands to rest and poverty will come on you like a bandit and scarcity like an armed man.

Proverbs 24:30-34

What time did you get up this morning?

That's a question I have often answered with reluctance and embarrassment because the answer might have been, "9, 9:30, 10." My standard defense has been, "I'm a night owl," while acknowledging that I "need" 8 to 9 hours of sleep each night.

I jokingly say that if not for my propensity to sleep late, I probably would have resolved the conflict in the Middle East by now. How much could I have achieved in the one to three hours each morning I should have been awake?

For the last 12 years, I have had jobs that did not require me to get to work at a certain hour and for the last 12 years I have struggled to get up out of bed and to work before restaurants stop serving breakfast. I redeem myself somewhat by being a hard worker with the ability to stay at a task with great concentration and attention and by working long hours into the evening when most of my co-workers are at leisure and home.

The last couple of years, my schedule went something like this: wake at 9, start working by noon, work until 8 or 9 p.m., wind down with the family and hit the hay at midnight or later. I rationalized that if I adjusted everything by about three hours, it would be the regular working woman's schedule. But in deep recesses of my mind, I knew my routine was hindering my productivity and my physical and emotional health.

100   By the time I woke up, the rest of the world was already in motion and as I would try to exercise or read my Bible and pray, the phone was ringing, barking dogs wanted in and out, and my family needed my attention. This, in turn, left me feeling frustrated throughout the day, as I would try to carve out a time to get back to those important yet not urgent things on my to-do list.

Shortly after I turned 40 (yes, 40 long years it took me to determine this!), I decided to "grow up" and join the rest of the world on its schedule. I decided to discipline myself to wake up early, start work at a certain hour, end at a certain hour (excepting right before deadlines), and get to bed by 11 p.m. I decided I do not need more than eight hours of sleep and would find that my body would adjust if I would just hold fast to a bedtime for a few months. I made this decision because I wanted to get more out of my day. I wanted an exercise routine for my health, I wanted quiet time with God, I wanted to be a better teacher to my daughter and I needed more time at work. I knew the benefits would be many and significant.

They say deciding to do something is half the battle, but I'm here to tell you the other half of the battle is the most grueling! Sleep is a formidable foe and very stealthy. Even Jesus acknowledged how powerful sleep is when He said, "The spirit is willing but the body is weak" (Mark 14:38).

Early on, I realized I could not go this alone. I asked God for help in this discipline and He has been faithful to wake me up every single morning without an alarm clock at just the time I would need to get out of bed to get it all done in a day. On the days I've ignored my heavenly wake-up call, I've found that if I had just gotten out of bed when I first woke up, instead of rolling over and sleeping another half hour or more, I would have been able to do that very thing I did not get done.

For me, being fair, honest and generous, trusting God and being grateful – all at once – is a piece of cake compared to getting out of bed on time! Nevertheless, I can't give up because physical discipline is extremely important. Almost every truly successful person is also a physically disciplined person. Highly successful people exercise regularly, wake up early, work long hours and balance work with family, hobbies and relaxation. Beyond the earthly benefits, becoming physically disciplined is God's will for us. As we mature in our walk of faith, God will reveal to us that to honor Him we need to eat right, maintain our weight and hygiene, exercise regularly (unless we have a physically demanding job) and relax and rest regularly – one of the reasons for which He established the sabbath (Exodus 31:12-17).

Clearly, this is no lecture on how to achieve physical discipline, as I am still trying to dig myself out of the ditch. What I can say is that it is hard yet worthwhile and that if you ask God to help you, with whatever it may be – exercise, diet, waking early – God is a very good helper.

Hold this thought: Eight hours of sleep is enough. I have more important things to do than sleep.

Start a Moss Collection Today

The wise woman builds her house, but with her own hands the foolish one tears hers down.

Proverbs 14:1

Do you know the expression, "a rolling stone gathers no moss?" It means that if you keep moving, you won't accumulate excess baggage – stuff and things. Well, as it turns out, moss can be a good thing. Moss can be resources – both tangible and intangible – and we, as women, need to roll into one place and start collecting some of it. If we stay in the same house, city, relationship and job, we have a better chance at gathering the things we want in life than if we roll from one house, relationship or job to another.

Change can be good if it means upward mobility. It's OK to change jobs if we're moving from one right into another that pays better and builds our skills and resume. It's OK to move from an apartment into our own home. And it's great to sell that first home for a profit and move into a larger home. These are upward moves and they actually help us accumulate moss.

Yet often, we make moves not upward, but sideways or down, and sometimes we make them out of sheer boredom. The mobile character of our society breeds restlessness in us, making it harder to stay with something after the excitement has worn off completely. When we come to that point, instead of allowing our attention to be pulled to something new and exciting, we need to dig in our heels of commitment and remember how much we appreciated what we have when we first got it, how useful and good in our lives it currently is and how making a change will drain us of resources that we cannot afford to lose.

Constant wanting and acting to satisfy those wants – for a

102

new car, new job, new clothes – will drain a person of resources. A constant wanting for material things has negative consequences, no doubt. They are mild, however, compared to how a woman can undo her progress and limit her own opportunity in life by being restless in romance.

Even without children, divorce is painful and costly and despite what we may have heard, a woman usually comes out on the losing end of it. Except for those cases in which a woman is breaking away from an abusive spouse, divorce is a negative and devastating thing in a person's life. The financial toll is the least of it. The real cost is emotional. And sadly this undoing often grows from the seed of discontent, tended and fed until it destroys what was once the most precious thing in a woman's life.

103

One of the best financial plans we can make for ourselves, one of the best ways to ensure happy golden years, is to choose a husband wisely and then remain in that marriage. Should feelings of "I could do better" begin to ignite, we must quickly stamp them out as if they were sparks that could destroy our whole life by fire. We can't allow ourselves to be entranced by the ephemeral beauty of those sparks of discontent, allowing them to start a small flame which, out of fascination, we watch as it grows, thinking to ourselves, "I can put this out whenever I want." In an instant, we can lose control of the fire we allowed to start and it will destroy our home and family – all for a little fascination because we were bored.

It is a great skill to be able to appreciate the same old things anew each day. It's called stability and with it we will gather lots of the right kind of moss.

Hold this thought: I make calculated moves to better my life.

Laptop Envy

A heart at peace gives life to the body, but envy rots the bones.
Proverbs 15:30

104

The other day, my preteen daughter told me again (I've lost count how many times this makes) that she wanted a cell phone of her own. Besides the fact that she's so young, what makes this request so ridiculous is that she is almost constantly with either me or her father and we both have cell phones and allow her unlimited use. She almost always does have a cell phone. Clearly, it isn't the necessity that's driving the desire. It's that her friend Hannah has one.

The preteen's case for a cell phone sounds silly, but if we would look carefully at some of our desires, they might seem just as silly. For example, I want a laptop computer. On the surface, it doesn't seem to be such an unreasonable desire. My business requires heavy daily use of a computer. I haven't purchased a computer since June 2000 (which in technology years makes my computer about 1,000 years old – though through updates and additions, I'm able to run the newest software at a reasonable processing speed). And what's worse is that each time I power up a message comes on the screen that says, "Imminent hard drive failure is detected," – I kid you not! Then it gives me two options, pressing F1 to continue or F10 for set-up. The first time I saw that message, choosing between F1 and F10 felt like a life or death decision. I selected F1 and found that my computer functioned normally. And so now I see the doomsday message, select F1 and use the computer despite the dark cloud of imminent failure hanging over my head. I make regular back-ups so that I won't lose too much if ever that imminent time arrives.

To top it all off, I love to travel and do take more vacation than the average American, but not half as much as I would take if I could make them working trips. Having a laptop would enable me to do more of something I love: travel.

Have I not made a compelling case for a laptop?

There's just one square peg that won't fit: I have a functioning computer. I don't need another computer.

When I strip away all the points in my case for buying a laptop, I see that if one thing were different, I wouldn't even want a laptop. That one thing is that everyone else is getting one – in addition to their desktops. My aunt, who doesn't even work a traditional job, has one. My cousin has one – he's a massage therapist! Even my 18-year-old exchange student bought one before she left the States to go back to Colombia. People around me everywhere have something they don't need. I certainly don't need it less than they don't, so shouldn't I have it too?

And it's so easy to own one. Dell will give me 12 months of financing with no interest. For about $60 a month, I can own a laptop without paying a penny of interest!

Yet my mind keeps wandering back to that one wet blanket: I have a functioning computer. I don't need another computer.

Why? Why am I plagued by this reality check when it could be so easy for me to have what I want, what everyone else has and something I would put to good use?

That's Wisdom sitting on my shoulder gently prodding me to examine my real motives in wanting to buy a laptop right now. She's right. It's envy. I want to keep up with the Joneses.

> When I strip away all the points in my case for buying a laptop, I see that if one thing were different, I wouldn't even want a laptop. That one thing is that everyone else is getting one.

But you know what? I'm not in competition with the Joneses or my aunt or my cousin or my exchange student. This "race" of life is me against me. I heard a young swimmer once say, "When you swim, you're not racing anyone but yourself – your own best time." And that is the truth about life. We may be in lanes next to other swimmers, both fast and slow and maybe we can't help but check where we are in relation to them, but that really has nothing to do with our own personal best performance. If the swimmer next to me is going slow, it does not enable me to go faster and vice versa. In every situation, I have to assess only if I'm doing what I need to be doing to perform my best.

Being content with what I have is part of my personal best. It's important to me to not get sucked up into a consumer whirlwind in which I imagine needs that are not real. It's important for a lot of reasons, the least of which is good financial management and the greatest of which is that material things have a way of clogging up the soul and spirit.

God promises to meet our needs and God wants to give us the desires of our hearts too. When we seek God first, He will provide all of that – that's one of God's promises to us. If we allow our focus to shift time and again from God's way to our next inessential gadget acquisition, we'll never find satisfaction. When we get what we want, we'll want something else. Nothing finally satisfies our craving for material things. It will consume us like a mold until even our bones are rotten.

Hold this thought: I am not competing with anyone in life.

The Boob Tube

When you sit to dine with a ruler, note well what is before you, and put a knife to your throat if you are given to gluttony. Do not crave his delicacies for that food is deceptive.

Proverbs 23:1-2

Do not let your heart envy sinners, but always be zealous for the fear of the Lord.

Proverbs 23:17

Yesterday I got my *Drew Magazine*, the alumni relations publication of my Alma Mater. Each time one arrives in the mail, I look forward to flipping to the back where the updates on alumni by class are located. It's always a bit of a thrill to get news about someone I haven't even given a second thought in years. Even more so when I read something about someone I have been thinking of. The kind of thing people get off their haunches to write in about are most often marriages, additions to the family, big moves and new jobs.

However, I have to be careful when I read *Drew* because I tend to become a little discouraged afterward. It's great to see what some folks have been up to, but it can create in me feelings of competition, desperation – like time is running out for me – and yep, envy and jealousy.

One of the great things about living in rural Arkansas is that most of our neighbors have fairly simple tastes. You don't see fancy sports cars driving down gravel roads. The only kind of art that people seem to be concerned about collecting is the kind that sits in the yard. The "elite" are the doctors and lawyers of the town and there's only one big social event of the year – the New Year's Eve party sponsored by Ducks Unlimited (I kid you not). And we have no mall!

It's not hard here in rural Arkansas to keep my mind off of material things because, relatively speaking, not many people have them. It's very liberating and saves my family a ton of money – especially when it comes to our preteen. Every once in a while she needs a Limited Too fix, but more often, she's content to try to find what she needs at Goodwill first.

But when *Drew Magazine* arrives, out comes the measuring stick. How am I doing compared to so and so? Married – check! Kids – check! Recent promotion – check! New home – check! Wait, what's this? Trip to Cairo? Waaa! Why don't I get to go to Cairo? I never get to go to Africa! Oh the inequality of it all!

Silly, huh? You don't do that? Good for you and don't ever fall into that trap.

Life is not a race against other people. It's a marathon and I am the only runner (yes, another sports analogy). The object is to finish and run well, not to get to the end first – Dear God, no, I don't want to finish the course in record time! I want to take my time, appreciate the scenery I'm trotting by and at the end have some memories of fun things that happened along the way. And what is the point of accumulating a lot of baggage you can't take across the finish line? When we cross that line, we have to leave everything except for the relationships we formed – they will follow us into eternity.

Some say, "I can't take it with me, but I can have fun with it while I'm still here." There's a well-hidden truth about stuff and things – the more you have of them the more complicated your life gets. Our most recent "toy" acquisition is proof of this principle.

After my husband got out of the Navy, he went to college at the ripe old age of 37. From the time he first enrolled, we've been motivating him by dangling a big-screen, high-definition television as a carrot to keep him going. This year he finally graduated and it was time to purchase that long-awaited graduation gift, the big TV. We got an LG (ironically stands for Life is Good) 60-inch plasma. It came highly recommended. Good-bye little 27-inch fat, box TV we bought at a pawn shop five years ago for $75. Hello $1,900 brand spanking new big boy. This thing is so monstrous we had to remodel to make a space for it! We put it in the basement and as soon as we did, we felt the need to put another lock on the door now that we have something worth stealing.

We brought the big boy home in mid April, about a month before my husband actually graduated. The week before his graduation and the big party in which he was going to show off his graduation gift to our friends and neighbors, the TV stopped working. It would turn on then shut itself off instantly. We called to have it repaired and it had to be taken away – for two weeks! On the day of our party, we stuck a 13-inch TV in the spot where the big boy had been, just for kicks. I told my husband, "God let you have it, but He wasn't about to let you flaunt it!"

About a week later, we welcomed the big boy back from the TV hospital and it was so nice to see it back in place. Move aside you 13-inch runt – the big boy is back!

A few weeks later, we were watching a movie and guess what? The TV started doing its thing again – shutting off as soon as it was turned on. This time LG said they would replace it instead of repair it. So we loaded the big boy up and drove it 90 miles to the nearest mega electronics store, returned it and got a new one. Because they didn't have another of the model we had purchased, they gave us the newer model and LG picked up the majority of the price difference, though we had to pay $150 more. Back home, installed again, and finally, in July – three months after we first brought the original big boy home – the TV situation seems to be squared away.

By way of comparison, our 27-inch pawn shop TV and the

little 13-incher have never given us a moment of grief. The big boy complicated our lives and for what? A widescreen? It's hardly worth it – we still have those annoying black bands at the top and bottom of this screen when we watch most movies! And now after trying a couple of different cables, we learn that we need a new DVD player to get the real high definition effect with this big TV. Oh bother!

Sadly, I could provide dozens of similar examples about how bigger and more has complicated my life. The delicacies of the material world are indeed deceptive. We think they make life more enjoyable and easier, but it's not true. There's nothing more fun than swimming in a lake or the ocean – why would I want the pain in the neck of the weekly maintenance required to have my own pool? You can't beat taking a brisk walk or jog in the great outdoors for the mental and physical health benefit, so why would I want a space-consuming treadmill to stub my toe on in the middle of the night?

The lure of material possessions and keeping pace with other people overrides common sense. Stop the nonsense before it starts! Don't have a lot of material possessions now? Don't waste your energy and money trying to acquire them. So what if all your friends have them. Go over to their houses and use theirs. Go swim in your neighbor's pool or watch TV on your neighbor's big screen. You get all the benefit without any of the cost or hassle and you save your money for things that are more important like living within your means, for starters. With all the money you save you can have a reliable car, a comfortable home, and a college fund for your kids (in the future), and you'll able to "be generous on every occasion," which is the real reason God has blessed you (check it out - II Corinthians 9:11).

Hold this thought: My life is good because I keep it simple.

For a Real Eye-Opener, Count Sheep

Be sure you know the condition of your flocks, give careful atten-
tion to your herds; for riches do not endure forever, and a crown is
not secure for all generations. When the hay is removed and new
growth appears and the grass from the hills is gathered in, the
lambs will provide you with clothing, and the goats with the price
of a field. You will have plenty of goats' milk to feed you and your
family and to nourish your servant girls.

Proverbs 27:22-27

We think of the Proverbs as being full of practical advice, but
have you paused to reflect that it contains a lot of promises
too? This verse is a great blend of advice and promise – and just
what I needed after working on my budget recently.

I made a budget about a year ago and for several months, we
stuck to it well and saw the results – we paid off debt and were
able to afford some luxuries. Gradually, our resolve to comply
with the budget wore thin and not coincidentally, we began
to have bigger and bigger credit card bills, carrying debt over
from one month to the next until it started to scare us and we
needed an intervention to figure out what to do about it.

So it was back to the budget. My husband and I sat down
and figured our income first. We felt pretty good about that;
both of us are making more than we ever have (although I'm
not sure that would remain true if we adjusted for inflation).
Then we started listing the expenses, beginning with tithes and
offerings. When we had most of them down, the major ones
we could easily think of, we did a subtotal and still had a lot of
money left at the end of the month. Still felt pretty good. Then,
as we chewed on our pencils, we started thinking of other expenses. Every couple of minutes, a new expense would come
to mind. Before we knew it, we had whittled down that couple

of thousand left over to just a couple of hundred left over. What a bummer!

This just wouldn't do, because we hadn't yet budgeted for birthdays, holidays or vacations and we had only a minimal amount for retirement savings. So we decided to conduct an analysis of the way we spend. We recorded all our expenses in one month to determine if our budget numbers were accurate and to see if perhaps we were spending money on some things we really didn't need – which was surely the case.

When my husband got a full-time job after having been a student for three and a half years and employed only part time, we thought we were going to have a nice margin of comfort between income and expenses. However, before we took stock of our flocks and herds, we went out and bought a new field – a Honda Element – and financed it for only three years, which is good in that we end up paying less in interest, but not so good in that our payments are high. Now, we're facing a tough three years financially while we pay the car off at the same time that I'm investing money in my business. We rushed in adding flocks to the herds and now they're running amok!

Attending to our flocks and herds is a pretty depressing endeavor, to be honest, but oh so necessary. We have goals: paying off debt, retirement savings, and getting our neglected teeth fixed! But we'll never get there if we don't pay attention to our flocks and herds. Oh, but look at the promise that awaits us if we will stay the course: the lambs will keep clothes on our backs and the goats will provide enough for us

If we're nickeling and diming away an income of $1,200 a month and we're depressed about it, think how we would feel if we started to nickel and dime away an income of $2,400, $3,600, $4,800 or more.

to invest in new ventures. We'll have enough to meet our own needs and the needs of my employees.

Are finances a huge issue for you? Newsflash: You're not alone! I don't think there's a person alive who doesn't need to heed the advice in this verse. If it seems hard to manage with only a few flocks – not even really a herd to speak of – wait until they increase! The truth is that the more flocks we add, the more herds that accumulate, the more important it is to keep a good handle on them. As our income and wealth increases, so does the potential to mismanage. If we're nickeling and diming away an income of $1,200 a month and we're depressed about it, think how we would feel if we started to nickel and dime away an income of $2,400, $3,600, $4,800 or more. We've got to get a handle on flock and herd management while we have only a few, then as they increase, we'll have the know-how and the good habits in place to enjoy the income and wealth that we've earned.

Another thing that comes with more flocks and herds is the potential to lose them to the wolves. Today's wolves come in a lot of different clothing; we often don't recognize them and we may even help the wolves: signing up for programs with recurring billing that we forget we signed up for and never use; buying unnecessary insurance coverage; overpaying for a product because we didn't shop around; paying for tax preparation when we use the 1040-EZ form (c'mon!). The more money in our budget, the greater the chance we'll throw it away on some of these and other financial wolves.

What we have to do is stay actively engaged in money management. All too often and in too many areas of life, we can find ourselves drifting off course, ignoring the waving red flags as we're floating carelessly along. We've got to snap out of it and take control of our course. If we feel like, "I'm not getting anywhere financially," then we need to ask, "Where is it we're trying to go?" Do we know? Have we set financial goals for ourselves? Do we have it on paper or on the computer? Have we looked to see if each month we're bringing in more money than we're spending and if so, what we're doing with the leftover money? If not, it's time to start counting sheep.

Hold this thought: I will live from a budget.

Love Your Co-Signer as Yourself

My daughter, if you have put up security for your neighbor, if you have struck hands in pledge for another, if you have been trapped by what you said, ensnared by the words of your mouth, then do this, my daughter, to free yourself, since you have fallen into your neighbor's hands: Go and humble yourself; press your plea with your neighbor! Allow no sleep to your eyes, no slumber to your eyelids. Free yourself, like a gazelle from the hand of the hunter, like a bird from the snare of the fowler.

Proverbs 6:1-5   **115**

As we emerge into the adult financial world, we find that transacting for big things, like the purchase of a car or leasing an apartment, require credit and resources that are difficult for a young person to obtain. How can we build credit if no one will give us credit, right?

Recognizing this conundrum, financial institutions have come up with the concept of the co-signer – that's bank-speak for "someone equally responsible to pay the obligation." A co-signer or guarantor on a loan or a lease might as well be taking out the loan or lease him or herself. If we should need a co-signer, we should ask the very closest person to us with good credit. We will get a chilly reception asking that rich aunt or uncle whom we only see at Christmas to take on our financial obligations. Co-signing is not just putting your name on a piece of paper, it is fully assuming the legal responsibility for the debt of another person – and our relative with good credit already knows this. Whereas we may need a co-signer we shouldn't dare become one until much later in life when we're financially secure. I repeat: Don't dare become a co-signer!

Mutual unconditional love needs to exist between co-signers. A co-signer is agreeing to pay the entire balance of the obligation – this is their unconditional love. If we know they cannot afford to do that without putting their own finances in jeopardy, we shouldn't even ask them, no matter how good their credit or how bad our predicament – this is our unconditional love. That same love will also compel us to meet our payment schedule and not do anything to jeopardize our loved one's credit. In these best of scenarios, co-signing can work, but what happens when there's love lost between co-signers?

When my father was in his 20s, he started an appliance and electronics retail sales business in a small town in Texas. In this depressed little town, many people wanted to buy his goods but few could afford to purchase them outright. This was back in the days before in-store financing and personal credit cards became ubiquitous. The only way to get a refrigerator, for instance, from Andy's was to pay cash or get a loan. Anxious to make the sale, make his business a success and feed his family of five, my father used his good credit to enable his customers to make purchases. He co-signed on the loans they took out to purchase his goods. It doesn't take a World Bank economist to figure out how risky that was, but somehow at the time it made sense to my dad, who is ironically a very intelligent man.

You can guess what happened next. His customers figured out that if they didn't make their loan payments, Andy would have to and there was nothing illegal about that. Andy was treating the whole town to televisions, stereos and appliances. Before long, Andy declared bankruptcy which put immeasurable stress on his marriage (which later fell apart) and necessitated moving his family and leaving the home he built with his own hands to go to the big city where he could get a job.

Do you think any of those people with the televisions and refrigerators lost a night's sleep about what happened to Andy's family? I don't. They didn't love us; their lives were not intricately entwined with ours. They were our neighbors, but, however close, they were no substitute for family. In short, co-signing can really mess us up!

So how do we reconcile Solomon's warning against co-signing for a neighbor with instructions Jesus gives in the New Testament? Jesus says, "Love your neighbor as yourself" (Matthew 22:39), and "Give to everyone who asks" (Luke 6:30).

I believe Jesus wants us to be generous and give wisely – giving what is really needed (which might not be what is asked for) and giving what we are able to give without violating God's principles by putting ourselves in debt or a bad way with our own creditors.

117

When we don't feel it is wise to give what's being asked – for any of a variety of reasons – we can give something else. If we ask God how we can help, God will show us resources we may not have realized we have that can be of help in our neighbor's time of need. As Christ said, we shouldn't refuse anyone who asks of us, but that doesn't mean we have to give that person literally what she asked for. Can we help our neighbor find a social services organization that can assist? How about helping by giving of time? Maybe our neighbor needs someone to watch her kids while she goes out on a job search.

Resourcefulness is better than good credit. The more of it we give, the more we have ourselves. As we find resources to meet the needs of others, we add to our own repertoire of resources for the future.

When asked to give, don't say "no." Give something, but don't give away your good name and credit. Give wisely, being generous with resourcefulness.

Hold this thought: I can always give something – but not my good credit.

I Want it All...Eventually

Better to be a nobody and yet have a servant than pretend to be somebody and have no food.

Proverbs 12:9

One woman pretends to be rich, yet has nothing; another pretends to be poor, yet has great wealth.

Proverbs 13:7

One of the hardest things about the transition to being on our own is the realization that we can't have everything we want right now. Delaying gratification is made even more difficult in our credit-based economy. Credit card companies are willing to extend $1,000 of credit even if we don't have a job. This may seem like just the solution we need to be able to afford a sofa or the latest cell phone or MP3 player, a laptop computer – or whatever it is we are craving. However hard it is for us to accept, we are better off going without a phone at all than to go into debt to buy one.

Purchasing almost anything on credit makes it less of a value. Why? Because once interest is added, we end up paying more for it than it is worth. Nonetheless, there are some purchases worth going into debt for. A good financial rule of thumb is that we should never go into debt for anything that does not increase in value over time. There are only a handful of things that meet this criterion: real estate, classic cars and other antiques and some collectibles, like coins or stamps. But who wants to go into debt for antiques and coins? That leaves us with real estate.

Did you know that if you were to buy a $100,000 house at a low interest rate of five percent and pay for it over 30 years, without factoring in taxes or insurance, in the end you will have paid $193,255 for the house? That very low interest rate of five percent makes a $93,255 difference over time. Think how an interest rate of eight, 12 or 19 percent – rates more common to credit cards – could swell a debt with time. Nonetheless, the purchase of a house, for example, is usually worthwhile because when those same 30 years have passed, the value of the house may have doubled or even tripled. By the time we finish paying $193,255 for the house, it could be worth $250,000 and we will have come out ahead. We made an investment by borrowing money to buy a house. We still paid more for it than we would have had we paid cash, but most people can't save enough money to buy a house outright and all that time we're working on saving money to own a house, we would likely be throwing away our money on rent. Because it's a big ticket item that we will have to spend money on regardless of whether we own it or not, it is reasonable and even smart to go into debt for a place to live.

Let's contrast that with the purchase of a car.

A car is almost essential in many parts of the United States, and therefore can almost be a justifiable reason to take on a big debt. If we have a steady source of income and we've worked out our budget and know that we can afford the car payment, the insurance, about $100 a month for upkeep (yes, it *does* cost that much on average, even on a newer car) and the fuel to run it, buying a car on payments, though not the best decision, may be worthwhile.

The best way to purchase a car is to save money and pay for the car outright. This requires a lot more forethought than most people give to buying a car – it requires saving for years. Even if we just bought a car, if we will start saving now for our next car, we may be able to purchase a car with cash – the best way – next time around.

So what kind of car do we want now? We're wise gals; we

don't want to go crazy, but we would like a nice new car that we don't have to worry about. Ah yes, a Honda Civic. For the sake of this example, let's say we find a Honda Civic for $20,000 (a nice round number) and we get that same good interest rate of five percent and set up payments for five years, which is typical. When we make our last payment, we will have paid a total of $22,645 for that car that is now only worth about $10,000 – and that's a best case scenario in which we sell it ourselves. If we want to trade our five-year-old Civic in on a new car, the dealer might offer us $6,000 if the car is in good shape.

120

For our hypothetical house, we paid $193,255 for something worth $250,000 when we finally paid it off. For our hypothetical car, we paid $22,645 for something worth, at best, $10,000 when we finally paid it off. Real estate appreciates, or gains value, over time. Cars, cell phones, music collections, beanie babies, furniture, electronics and clothes all depreciate, or lose value, over time. The purchase of anything that loses value over time is *never* an investment and should, therefore, not be financed (bought on credit). A big ticket essential like a car, may have to be an exception, especially if having one is the only way to get you to a job. Smaller items like furniture, electronics and clothes should never be bought on credit.

So what's a gal to do? First of all, we just have to settle into the realization that we're just starting out and that means there are some things for which we'll have to wait and work. That's such a hard pill to swallow, but it might help to think of these as our lean and hungry years. We can imagine ourselves as great artists who are gaining material and motivation by a little suffering during this period in our life and development as an artist. These are the years that give us the depth of character we'll need to portray that famous dramatic role or to paint the lines of suffering on a weather-worn face. Lean and hungry years don't last that long if we are wise with our money. If we are not, if we try to circumvent lean and hungry years by having everything we want now, on credit, we'll only prolong our lean and hungry years. Our whole life can end up lean and hungry if we're not careful to avoid debt on things that lose value.

OK. We're lean and hungry, but that doesn't mean starving! We've got to tap our resources. Let people know what we need and maybe they can help us. And we shouldn't wait until we're sitting on the floor of our new apartment to start asking. Put the word out three months in advance to give people a chance to work around to it. Don't expect to get a free cell phone, but someone we know may be just about ready to get new furniture and if they know we need furniture, they may pass their old stuff on to us. Hey, it's better than sitting on the floor!

121

Shop garage sales, Goodwill, Salvation Army and church thrift stores. My local Goodwill has a dedicated Abercrombie rack!

If we've exhausted our friends, family and second-hand store options and we still can't find what we're looking for, we may just have to go without it. What? No cell phone? No laptop? Well, not yet.

If we want something like a cell phone that is a recurring monthly expense, we should think about how we could trim money from our current expenses. Could we shop for clothes only at second-hand stores and afford a cell phone payment this way? Could we do our own nails? How about living in a smaller apartment? If we can't cut expenses, maybe we can add income. Can we work a few hours a week more with a weekend or evening job?

We may have thought of

> It might help to think of these as our lean and hungry years. We can imagine ourselves as great artists who are gaining material and motivation by a little suffering during this period in our life.

all of this and be doing it all and still not be able to afford something we really want. And there waits credit – so graciously extended to us! Why not? We think, "I can't afford $900 to buy the laptop with cash, but I can afford $30 a month credit card payment." This is dangerous thinking. It may be true, and if that laptop can help us earn more money or decrease our spending in some significant way, it might be worth it. Recall, however, that with credit card interest rates we will be paying more for the laptop than it's worth. Do the math. (I did mine on www.engineersedge.com/calculators/credit_card.htm using 15 percent interest with minimum payments of $30 a month.) Buying a laptop on credit will make us the sucker who spent $1,135 on a $900 laptop that is worth about $300 by the time we get it paid off.

Don't be a sucker for instant gratification. Swallow the hard pill of delayed gratification, stay out of debt and let's get our lean and hungry years over with quickly.

Hold this thought: I am satisfied with what I have.

chapter five

When Morality Meets Reality

A Righteous Babe

A Righteous Babe Remix

Easy Money? Think Again.   123

Bunny Killers Brought to Justice

The Progressive Pizza Puke

Hiding Behind Cloth

The Pursuit Counts for Something

I Wouldn't Touch it with a 10-Foot Pole

Marked for Life

The Speed Trap

Good for the Soul

The Tapestry of Justice

A Righteous Babe

Ill-gotten treasures are of no value, but righteousness delivers from death.
The Lord does not let the righteous go hungry but he thwarts the craving of the wicked.

Proverbs 10:2-3

Blessings crown the head of the righteous, but violence over-whelms the mouth of the wicked.
The memory of the righteous will be a blessing, but the name of the wicked will rot.

Proverbs 10:6-7

What the wicked dreads will overtake him; what the righteous de-sire will be granted.
When the storm has swept by, the wicked are gone, but the righ-teous stand firm forever.

Proverbs 10:24-25

The prospect of the righteous is joy, but the hopes of the wicked come to nothing.
The righteous will never be uprooted, but the wicked will not re-main in the land.
The lips of the righteous know what is fitting but the mouth of the wicked only what is perverse.

Proverbs 10:28, 30, 32

The righteousness of the blameless makes a straight way for them, but the wicked are brought down by their own wickedness.
The righteousness of the upright delivers them, but the unfaithful are trapped by evil desires.

Proverbs 11:5-6

The righteous man is rescued from trouble and it comes on the wicked instead.

Proverbs 11:8

The wicked man earns deceptive wages, but he who sows righteousness reaps a sure reward.

Proverbs 11:18

The desire of the righteous ends only in good, but the hope of the wicked only in wrath.

Proverbs 11:23

125

The plans of the righteous are just, but the advice of the wicked is deceitful.

Proverbs 12:5

The light of the righteous shines brightly, but the lamp of the wicked is snuffed out.

Proverbs 13:9

Misfortune pursues the sinner, but prosperity is the reward of the righteous.

Proverbs 13:21

The Lord is far from the wicked, but he hears the prayer of the righteous.

Proverbs 15:29

Whoa! That was a lot of Proverbs at once. Are you still with me?

I always had a little trouble wrapping my mind around the concept of righteousness until one day I was reading the Bible in Spanish – the verse, "seek ye first the kingdom of God and its righteousness…" – and I saw that the word "righteousness" in Spanish was "justicia," which translated back to English means "justice." Now "justice" is a much easier concept for me and probably for most people, especially young people since we learn very early on to evaluate situations as "fair" or "not fair."

The dictionary defines "righteous" as "just or fair, doing the right thing" and "good." It's really a very simple concept tied up in a big word. And yet, though we start learning this concept as toddlers, it continues to challenge us throughout life. Simple, yet complex for two main reasons: 1. The right thing is not always easy to figure out; and 2. When it is obvious, we don't always want to do the right thing.

Some things we know to be good and right, but we don't want to do them – like flossing or brushing our teeth before bedtime. If flossing is hard, how much more something like apologizing for a hurtful remark!

Other times, it is not so easy to decide which, among our limited options, is the right one. I bet you've already been in a bunch of situations in which you realize that regardless of what you decide to do, someone has to suffer, someone has to hurt, someone will not like you. These situations creep up all the time in adult life; they are not just reserved for major life crises.

I encountered one of these "what is right?" situations once when I found out that a teenager I knew smoked. He said his parents knew he smoked, but I doubted that was true because I couldn't imagine that his parents would allow him to smoke. What should I do: mind my own business and let that family take care of itself? Or should I butt in and tell the parents their kid

What should I do: mind my own business and let that family take care of itself? Or should I butt in and tell the parents their kid smokes?

smokes?

There didn't seem to be anything wrong with minding my own business – basically I would make no impact on the situation. I would not change things for better or for worse. Whereas if I told the parents, they might see me as a busybody; they might get defensive; and most certainly, the teenager would be ticked off at me.

That's the easy analysis – better mind my own business, right? What happens though when I apply the golden rule – do what you would want someone else to do if the situation were reversed?

If I were the parent of a teen who smoked and I didn't know he smoked, but some other parent did know, I would most certainly want that parent to tell me.

What about the teenager – doesn't the golden rule apply to him? True, if I were a teenager I wouldn't want someone to rat me out, but on the flip side, I would want someone to care enough about me to do something against my will but for my benefit even though she knew it would make me mad and perhaps mean the end of any friendship we had. I wouldn't appreciate that kind of care for a long time, but if that "ratting out" led to some intervention that stopped me from forming a life-long addiction to a destructive chemical that will rob me and my children of good health, I would eventually have to acknowledge that it was right thing to do. That's how I hope that teen will feel some years from now, because I ratted him out! And I bet you can guess the mother's reaction: she really appreciated me telling her.

Doing the right thing will not always make us feel happy and it certainly won't make us popular. I don't see a promise of feel-good or popularity anywhere in the proverbs above. But look what they say will come with righteousness (and this is just a partial list from the verses above):

- Delivery from death
- Our lives will be a sweet memory
- Desires granted
- Joyous prospects
- We'll be firmly rooted
- We'll know just what to say
- A straight path for us in life
- Rescue from trouble
- Sure reward
- Our desires will turn out well
- Our plans will remain just
- The light of our example will shine brightly
- Rewards of prosperity

and most importantly,

- The Lord will hear our prayers.

With all these advantages, it is really worthwhile to do the tough analytical work to figure out what is the good, just and right thing to do and, once that is clear, to just do it.

Hold this thought: When the right thing to do is not easy to figure out, apply the golden rule.

Righteous Babe Remix

Now when a woman works, her wages are not credited to her as a gift, but as an obligation. However, to the woman who does not work but trusts God who justifies the wicked, her faith is credited to her as righteousness.

Romans 3:4

I know, this isn't a proverb. I just want to visit one more aspect of "righteousness" as it applies to us today. Whereas we were talking about righteousness in the sense of doing the right thing, righteousness has another meaning as well. With the coming of Jesus Christ, his death and resurrection, a person is made righteous immediately with the simple act of believing in Christ as her personal savior.

Regardless of the mistakes we have made in life, the blatant wrong we may have willingly and even cheerfully committed, we are not doomed to "wicked" status. By simply deciding to commit our mind, soul and body to the belief that there is a God and that God sent His son Jesus to die and rise again, thus canceling out the power of sin over us for all time and that we as sinners need this redeeming power, we will become instantly righteous.

When we have faith in Jesus Christ and God our father, we are just and right with God, which is what Paul means in Romans 5:1, "Therefore, since we have been justified through faith, we have peace with God through our Lord Jesus Christ, through whom we have gained access by faith into this grace in which we now stand." The "grace" is our present state of being righteous in God's eyes.

Now what? Can we remain in a constant state of righteousness if we only believe? Well, yes. If we only believe and remain free of sin. Romans 6:1-3 in *The Message* says: "So what do we do? Keep on sinning so God can keep on forgiving? I should hope not! If we've left the country where sin [reigns], how can we still live in our old house there? Or didn't you realize we packed up and left there for good?"

The thing to do now is to keep our faith strong by consistently making the right choices that will keep our life free of faith-polluting influences. And this is where that tough analytical work I talked about in the last section comes into play.

I just wanted to make it perfectly clear that it is not the effort of doing the right thing that makes us right with God. What makes us right with God is our faith in God and His son Jesus. Faith in God establishes the right relationship with our Creator. To maintain our right relationship, we must maintain our faith. That maintenance requires the same kind of maintenance any relationship requires.

130

It's a righteousness cycle: We believe → God counts this as righteousness and calls us His daughter → we put forth the effort to be a good daughter → which, in turn, strengthens our relationship with our Father.

For a moment, let's compare our relationship with God to a friendship. What happens if we neglect to talk to a friend for days on end, and instead hang out with people who don't like that friend? We grow apart. The same will happen with our relationship with God.

Imagine God is our best friend and the evil influences of the world are a huge clique of "cool" people who have set about to destroy our friendship with God, who they consider to be a real geek. They want us to be one of them. At every opportunity, someone from the cool

> We can't spend time with God and the cool clique – they have irreconcilable differences, mainly one is life and the other is death.

clique is slinking up and whispering doubts in our ear: "What are you doing with that geek? You should be out having fun with us!" We start to think that it wouldn't hurt to hang out with the cool clique every now and then. So we give a try. But then our best friend finds out and He is hurt because He knows what the cool clique thinks of Him and that they want to break our friendship apart. So, yes, it hurts our relationship with God when we choose sin and evil over Him. It chips away at our faith in our best friend. We can't spend time with God and the cool clique – they have irreconcilable differences, mainly one is life and the other is death. We need to cling to our best friend, our Heavenly Father, to keep the relationship alive and healthy.

131

Read the proverbs on righteousness again and this time, insert the words, "faith in God" for "righteousness" and "the one who has faith in God" for "the righteous." And visualize yourself as that one.

Hold this thought: A strong relationship with God makes me right.

Easy Money? Think Again.

My daughter, if sinners entice you, do not give in to them. If they say, "Come along with us; let's lie in wait for someone's blood, let's waylay some harmless soul; let's swallow them alive, like the grave, and whole, like those who go down to the pit; we will get all sorts of valuable things and fill our houses with plunder; throw in your lot with us, and we will share a common purse" – my daughter, do not go along with them, do not set foot on their paths; for their feet rush into sin, they are swift to shed blood. How useless to spread a net in full view of all the birds! These people lie in wait for their own blood; they waylay only themselves! Such is the end of all who go after ill-gotten gain. It takes away the lives of those who get it.

Proverbs 1:10-19

Here's one of those passages in Proverbs that I skimmed over in my youth, dismissing as not applicable to me. Not only did I never hang out with people who would lay a trap to swallow someone alive like the grave, I was fairly sure I could resist the temptation if ever one of my friends concocted such an evil scheme. I wasn't wrong about any of that, but what I didn't consider is how this warning applies to the many ways that did come my way, and will come your way too, to make "ill-gotten gain" – that's a poetic phrase that encompasses any money or advantage that is not honestly earned or honestly received.

Most girls at some point or another have snuck into their mother's purse or father's wallet, and if it was possible to take a bill without it being too conspicuous, have done so. That's ill-gotten gain. How about going through the check-out at a store and knowing that the cashier did not charge us for an item. That has happened to me several times. Walking out of the store feeling like, "Score! Free stuff!" is ill-gotten gain.

132

If our parents have instructed and taught us correctly, just as soon as we walk away with our ill-gotten gain our conscience will start to tingle and will not let us rest until we either return it or make it right. Making it right is easy in both of the above scenarios, we just return the money or the merchandise. However, sometimes making it right is not so easy. Some things can't be made right, and then we have to live with the memory. For a short time, we may even feel good about what we got away with, but if we cannot make restitution for what we wrongly gained, we have set a trap of regret for ourselves that we cannot escape.

133

Temptation does not usually come to a person who is well-equipped to resist it. The opportunity for us to wrongfully acquire something will present itself at a particularly difficult time for us to resist. There was one such time in my life when money was very scarce, despite my honest efforts to control spending and work as much as I could.

One day I came upon a wallet sitting on a shelf in a K-Mart. I opened the wallet and saw two things, a $20 bill and a Medicaid card. The person who left this wallet on the shelf obviously needed both of these items back. I also needed money and walked right into a trap being set for myself as I reasoned that, even if I returned the wallet, no one could possibly know that I had taken the money out. I could say that only the Medicaid card was in it when I found it. How could anyone prove me wrong? No one could or ever did. I got a free $20 shopping spree at K-Mart that night and the owner of the Medicaid card presumably retrieved her wallet and card from the service desk.

I never bothered to focus on the name on the Medicaid card, so I have no idea from

> I never bothered to focus on the name on the Medicaid card, so I have no idea from whom I stole that money.

whom I stole that money. Many years later, my conscience is still tingling but I cannot make restitution for that ill-gotten gain even though I really would like to. Jesus Christ has forgiven me of that sin and does not hold it against me and I have even forgiven myself for throwing my lot in with the demons in my head. But I can never forget what I did and will always regret what I did. I would gladly give back 10 times the money I took to escape the ambush I set for myself on that desperate day.

Hold this thought: What I can't have honestly, I simply will not have.

Bunny Killers Brought to Justice

The woman of integrity walks securely, but she who takes crooked paths will be found out.

Proverbs 10:9

We all know that honesty is the best policy, but it is such a difficult policy to implement! Life gives us so many opportunities to better ourselves (temporarily) with a little bit of dishonesty. Many times, no other person is involved – it's us versus a corporation or government. We justify that they have so much and we, so little. We believe they are essentially unethical to profit so greatly often using dishonesty themselves, so a little of their own medicine is due them. There are innumerable justifications – so many to choose from!

135

Yet we know in our hearts that their dishonesty or unfair advantage over us, the little gal, does not make it right in the eyes of God for us to turn the tables on them. I know this very well, and yet I need reminders and sometimes, I need more than that. Sometimes I need God to force me to do the right thing for my own good.

One summer I rented a minivan for a family vacation across the country, from Arkansas to California. I didn't get the supplemental insurance; I never do, and I maintain that it is a waste of money when my own insurance or credit card provides comprehensive insurance coverage.

We were visiting national parks of the southwest and one that I wanted to see was the Mojave National Preserve – I wanted to camp there. We drove into the park as the sun was setting and went looking for the campground only to find that it had been destroyed by fire a few days earlier. This meant we had to drive out of the desert park at night to go looking for a hotel in a nearby city.

During the day the desert looks, well, deserted, but at night, a lot of creatures start to move around, and one in particular that likes to dart out in front of minivans to cross deserts roads is the jackrabbit. Without exaggeration, some 50 rabbits or more crossed in front of us on the short trip out of the Mojave Preserve. My husband has an odd philosophy about animals crossing the road which I can sum up by saying he doesn't slow down for them. We hit at least a dozen of those critters that night and it made for a very bumpy and disagreeable ride for this bunny lover.

136

Fast forward a few days to the dunes of Pismo Beach, Calif. As we ran down from the dunes back toward our minivan, we noticed that the front of the van below the bumper was uneven. Upon closer inspection, we found a very large jackrabbit resting in peace, lodged under the front spoiler. Under the stress of the big rabbit, the spoiler had cracked where it joined the bumper.

John and Donna's body shop open for business! We did not want to pay the $500 deductible for this damage. We reasoned that if we could fix the crack with putty and paint, it would be good as new and we wouldn't owe anything. After the third round of putty that didn't hold, we moved to plan B: give the van a good wash before we return it, prop the spoiler into place and hope they don't notice. This was the plan we were working under on our last day as we rushed homeward to wash the van and get it back before the rental deadline.

Throughout the days of puttying the crack and on our way home, I had a little devil and a little angel each camped on opposite shoulders, making their respective pitches to justify my plan and condemn it. Round about Oklahoma City, I finally reached up and flicked the angel off my shoulder – he was getting on my nerves so badly. I was going with the little devil's advice on this one. I guess I shouldn't have dissed the angel that way. I think it ticked him off. He got up, brushed himself off and flew out of the speeding van about a hundred feet ahead of us and then did an about-face and came charging at the van. I didn't see any of this, of course, I was whooping it up with the little devil.

But the angel got my attention when all of the sudden we heard a "pop" and we looked up and saw a big, bold crack in the windshield of our rental van! That diehard angel, bruised and battered, resumed his position on my shoulder and told the little devil to beat it – he was defeated. Then he said to me, "Hide that from the rental company!"

137

This was no laughing matter, but it didn't take very long for me to see the humor and irony in the situation and truly appreciate God's intervention to keep me honest. When I turned the minivan in, I filled out a damage report and noted both the cracked spoiler and the cracked windshield and went home with a clear conscience and grateful to God for a good, however expensive, reminder that honesty is the best policy.

Hold this thought: It's impossible to hide a lie forever.

The Progressive Pizza Puke

Wine is a mocker and beer is a brawler, whoever is led astray by them is not wise.

Proverbs 20:1

138

Who has woe? Who has sorrow? Who has strife? Who has complaints? Who has needless bruises? Who has bloodshot eyes? Those who linger over wine, who go to sample bowls of mixed wine. Do not gaze at wine when it is red, when it sparkles in the cup, when it goes down smoothly! In the end it bites like a snake and poisons like a viper. Your eyes will see strange sights and your mind imagine confusing things. You will be like one sleeping on the high seas, lying on top of the rigging. "They hit me," you will say, "but I'm not hurt! They beat me, but I don't feel it! When will I wake up so I can find another drink?"

Proverbs 23:29-35

One summer my preteen brother and sister came to stay a week with me while at the same time, my niece of the same age was also visiting. They had a lot of fun together and stayed up to the wee hours almost every night. Before they left, we took their film to be developed and among the pictures was a series of my little brother in various unconscious poses wearing broad strokes of lipstick. He had fallen asleep before the girls one night and they took the opportunity to poke fun at him by making up his face and taking pictures, which will be priceless for years to come.

The morning after their late-night mischief, my brother was not too happy and was even less so when he saw the pictures of him wearing big, colorful lips. He was humiliated by things he had unknowingly participated in. The girls added to the insult with generous commentary on how lovely he was!

Wine can do to a person what those girls did to my brother. And it's not just wine that can do it. They are not in the scriptures, but we can add to the list: tequila, gin, rum, vodka, whiskey and all other alcoholic drinks. Beer can make a fool of us, too, and I like how Solomon notes beer's specific quality of making people feel more aggressive and courageous than they have a right to. It does seem that of all the alcohols, beer is the base of more fights than any of the others.

When we read in this proverb, "whoever is led astray by them," we may be interpreting that to mean, "whoever becomes an alcoholic." However, we don't have to reach the extremes of addiction to have been officially "led astray." I'm no alcoholic, but I confess, I have most certainly been led astray by alcohol. By that I mean, in a drunken state, I have sinned and done things that, even if in themselves might not be considered sin, are completely humiliating and I would never want to see in a video replay – like vomiting a pitcher of Sangria in the sink of a restaurant, for instance. Yes, I know, that grossed you out. I wanted it to so you can understand the quality of memory a pitcher of Sangria promises.

For the fool, getting drunk is doubly "fun." First there's the getting drunk and the inane behavior that results. Secondly, there's the recounting of the tale numerous times in the days to follow, and if the debauchery resulted in something particularly stupid, the tale is good for weeks, months and even years to come.

If we continue to mature and want to do God's will more and more, there will come a time when those trophy stories become the skeletons in our closets.

Maybe we're thinking, "How fair is that, for someone else to have had all those crazy experiences but then to turn around and tell us that we shouldn't?"

That's a very valid argument if equity were the point. It's not though. The point is having an abundant life with as little heart-ache and regret as possible. I'm not recommending we deny ourselves fun or great memories. Instead, let's create memories worth preserving, while foregoing the kind that turn sour and rot in our minds. Let's spare ourselves from humiliation while we're having fun.

Maybe we don't care now about how some memory may not mesh with our lifestyles when we're a mother 15 years from now. To be that forward thinking is quite extraordinary. However, not all the memories one makes as a drunk take so long to ferment.

Just to make the point, I'll share one of mine (though I really would rather not). One night during my senior year of college, I ate a huge mess of pizza then went to a party in the hall of the first floor of the dorm where I lived (my room was on the fourth floor). It was a "golf party," in which at each of nine stations, or holes, we got a different kind of alcoholic drink; we marked our score cards (a check mark if we'd received our drink at a certain hole) and compared scores cards as we mingled. I did not complete the course before the hall began to spin. I had had too much and was feeling very sick very quickly. Sure, I was having a good time up until that point – or so it seemed. To be honest, I'm fuzzy on the details. I have a vague memory of it being fun though I cannot recall any specific situation to support that vague memory.

Regardless, the fun was over when the hall started to spin. I knew I had to get up to my room and quick. Before I made the second floor landing, I started to throw up. When the first retch-ing impulse stopped, I was able to climb another flight of stairs. Then, on the third floor, I threw up again on the stairs. With one last effort, I made it to the top and just outside my dorm room door, threw up one final time. Immediately humiliating? Yes, but that was only the beginning of the embarrassment.

Even though the dorm had housecleaning staff, for some reason, that awful mess was not cleaned up for an inordinately long time – like for some weeks. I wonder now at why I did not clean it up myself – well, I did clean the mess that was right outside my own door. It seems I didn't clean the other messes because I didn't want to admit to having made them, though my friends knew. I heard many people complain about the puke they had to endure as they came up and down the stairs. People on the fourth floor had to pass two messes coming and going! Worst of all, I had thrown up the pizza in layers. The crust was on the second floor, the tomato sauce on the third floor and the toppings had been right by my door. How's that for "glory days"?

141

My daughter often says, "Tell me a story about your college days." Do you know that I have almost run out of the ones suitable to tell her and mostly what I've got left are variations on the same pathetic theme of the Progressive Pizza Puke? What a shame.

Alcohol won't just mock us while we're drunk; it keeps on and keeps on mocking.

Hold this thought: I can have fun without being a fool.

Hiding Behind Cloth

To do what is right and just is more acceptable to the Lord than sacrifice.

Proverbs 21:3

Once I worked in a rented office space in a church. I hadn't worked there long when the pastor of the church wanted to have a little chat with me. He told me that he thought I should learn from him, versus from the inevitable grapevine, that he was being disciplined for a period of six months for having committed adultery. He had to have a window put in his office door and he was not supposed to be alone in the building with only one other woman (I was an exception because of the rental arrangement). He was very grateful to his parishioners that they had stood behind him and that his punishment was as light as it was.

We lived in a town where a lot of movies were filmed because of its beauty. One day, this minister met a woman from California who was in town with a film crew. I don't know any details beyond that except that it resulted in an affair. The minister thought it was over. He regretted it, told his wife, she forgave him and he hoped that would be the end of it. Then about a year later, the Californian was back in town for another film and she looked up her old flame. He wasn't interested though – he had regretted the first time. This didn't sit well with her and she tried to persuade him even through blackmail, which she went through with by making their affair public. The church leadership found out and the six-month discipline was the result.

This was strange news to get from a minister, a family man, a leader in the community. Until that Californian blew the whistle, this man was highly revered as a community role model. His congregation was very giving and sponsored and spurred on several social service initiatives for the poor and home-less. He walked around in black all day, with a reversed collar! He burned incense and listened to chanting monks! He held church services and Bible classes bunches of times weekly! His life was spent in service to the Lord and presumably the biggest sacrifice of all that he had made was using his gifted intellect in the Lord's service instead of using it to make himself rich. This was a man offering himself as a sacrifice to God on a daily basis. Yet how do you think God must have felt about all of that when he committed adultery?

In another conversation with that minister, he confessed to me that he had known as a youth that he had two courses in life: either to become a minister or to become a total reprobate. I understood through our years of conversation and my obser-vations of him that he struggled with lust.

One day, a friend of mine came to have lunch with me. My friend was a vivacious, petite Latina with thick, curly, long tress-es and who oozed sex appeal whether she meant to or not. We ate our lunch in the church kitchen. In comes the minister. Introductory platitudes gave way to chit chat which became lingering and eventually downright intrusive on our lunch. All the while, the minister was looking at my friend in a way that made me uncomfortable. When he left, she comment-ed on it too. How sick and how sad.

People often seek profes-sions to cure what ails them. I believe there to be a lot of wounded souls who are counselors, a lot of teachers who choose the profession because nobody respected

143

> In another conversation with that minister, he confessed to me that he had known as a youth that he had two courses in life: either to become a minister or to become a total reprobate.

or listened to them as kids and a lot of pastors who hide in the cloth because their alternative is to become a total reprobate. This is not a healthy rationale for selecting a profession. Much abuse can result from people seeking healing through their professions. It's risky business.

That's what's going on behind the scenes, in the depths of souls and psyches. In the foreground, however, we may see a life of service, a good and correct person – even a community role model. These people aren't always exposed, like so many abusive priests, counselors, nurses and teachers have been. We are fooled. But God is not fooled and we see in this proverb that he is not impressed. Foremost, God wants our hearts to be clean. When they are, we will do what is right and just, whether the act is visible or invisible, real or imagined.

Hold this thought: You can't judge a book by its cover.

The Pursuit Counts for Something

She who pursues righteousness and love finds life, prosperity and honor.

Proverbs 21:21

I don't want to leave you with the wrong impression about that minister I just told you about – the one who had an affair with the woman on the film crew from California. My final words were "You can't judge a book by its cover." And I want to reiterate that, but in a different sense. Don't believe for a second that just because that man's sin came to light that he is judged and condemned in God's eyes, jury's back; case is closed. No. Thank God, no! Life is more complex than that. Humans are more complex and certainly God is more complex than an open-and-shut case.

145

Whereas I may want to focus on the one time that minister screwed up big time, God takes it all into account when He makes His final call. What about all the time – an entire career – that minister spent about our Father's work, pursuing righteousness? Is it all for nothing because he struggles with lust? Is it effort in vain because he fell to temptation and committed adultery?

Please, don't answer those questions! They are rhetorical and not meant to be answered by anyone but God and He'll let us in on how He has decided on the final judgment day.

In our court system, when a person commits a crime, let's say shoplifting, she goes before a judge and will get one of two verdicts: guilty or not guilty. When the judge is making her decision, she doesn't take into consideration this person's grade point average and almost perfect attendance at school. She won't admit testimony from an elderly next-door neighbor about how this same young woman has gotten the old lady's cat out of the tree more than a dozen times. All those wonderful things count for nothing before this human judge who will make her decision based on the facts of the case and deem our shoplifter innocent or guilty, and her entire world with her, based on one incident. If she's found guilty, there will be a penalty and it if it's jail time, she will lose her job, her apartment, her car and anything else she's making payments on because a person has no substantial income in jail. Our young first offender's whole life has gone down the toilet. And we call this justice.

146

God defines justice differently though. God admits any and everything as evidence in His court room. Not only the testimonies of everyone who ever knew us, but all our actions, all our thoughts and all our intentions. He takes the entire person and all the circumstances into account and He doesn't need to sit through hours of boring exhibition – He knows it all already. Depending on the condition of our minds and hearts, that can either really work in our favor, or be pretty scary.

Another unique aspect of God's justice system is that if we hire the right attorney, we will always come away with a verdict of not guilty for any crime we commit. It's nepotism to the extreme because the attorney is the Judge's Son! His name is Jesus Christ and He only works pro bono. When we've committed an infraction of God's law, this attorney actually comes to our house, stands at the door and knocks, and if we will open the door, He comes in and has dinner with us. He puts our mind at ease, assuring us that what we did will not be held against us in God's court because we have Him as our attorney. And as if that isn't enough, He actually cleans our house and washes the windows! With all the clutter gone, we are new creatures and it seems even the way we think changes. Whatever insanity it was that caused us to shoplift in the first place is swept out of our lives.

Then, on that fateful day when we're in front of the Judge for the crime we committed, we are not thrown in jail. What our attorney promised us was true, we are found not guilty. But does that mean we get off scot-free? Not in God's court. Even with the Great Attorney, we still have to face consequences for our actions. We may come out with our liberty – free to enjoy eternal life – but the Bible says if we haven't lived right, we'll come through the judgment like a man rescued from the flames – all crispy charred and no hair (I Corinthians 3:15).

Those of us with friends or loved one who have committed a crime or one of those big, obvious sins like adultery, might be able to view that situation from a perspective similar to that of God's justice because we love the person who did wrong. I have a sister who was caught for shoplifting and thrown in the slammer. Although I know she was guilty in man's eyes, I still see a dear, sweet little girl in my mind's eye. I know how her childhood went wrong and the circumstances that produced a convict. My love for her is mercy and my love for her is also judgment because even if it were in my power to do so, I wouldn't withhold from her the consequences of her action. And so it is with God's love for us – the perfect balance of mercy and justice.

On the other hand, when I think of the crime of someone I don't know well or love dearly, like the adultery of the minister, I tend to want to apply man's judgment: He's guilty through and through. The consequences? A completely ruined witness. All he's ever done is a sham and all he'll ever do is a sham. That's my summary judgment.

But what about all that time the minister spent pursuing righteousness in earnest? What about the fact that he was so determined to flee from his devils that he chose a profession that he believed would safeguard him from them? Is that not earnest desire to live right? Doesn't all of that count for something?

It is rare that we can know God's judgment on a person in this life, but in His word, He has given us some case studies so we can see how complex His judgment is.

In the book of Kings and again in Chronicles, we see a rapid historical review of the kings of Judah and Israel. We have their names, lineage, number of years ruled, important details of their reign and God's final word on them. Most of them were big disappointments, but occasionally, seemingly out of no-where pops up a king who passes muster with God. King Asa was one of those. In I Kings 15:11-15, we have the case summary: "Asa did what was right in the eyes of the Lord... He expelled the male shrine prostitutes and got rid of the all the idols his fathers had made. He even deposed his grandmother Maacah from her position as queen mother, because she had made a repulsive Asherah pole. ... Although he did not remove the high places, Asa's heart was fully committed to the Lord all of his life."

148

In II Chronicles 14, 15 and 16, we get a lot more information about Asa. And again, the case summary starts off with these words: "Asa did what was good and right in the eyes of his God." Can we argue with that? When all was said and done, God has written in His word and twice said that in His very eyes, this man, Asa, did what was right. He calls him "fully committed to the Lord!" Wow. Asa certainly pursued righteousness, the man deposed his own grandmother! That's relentless pursuit of righteousness.

Think Asa ever did anything wrong? Well, we see in the scripture above that he did not remove the high places from Israel; these were idol temples that for some strange reason, he either didn't get around to removing or overlooked. Couldn't give Grandma a break, but he leaves the high places alone! Then, in the II Chronicles account, we find more dirt on Asa: In the 36th year of his reign – at an age he should have known better – he emptied the royal and holy treasuries to buy a political ally in a time of conflict with another kingdom. That irked God. The consequences? "You have done a foolish thing, and from now on you will be at war." Asa's reaction to his sentence wasn't exactly "good" or "right" either. He threw the messenger in jail and then "brutally oppressed some of the people." Then, at the end of his life, he came down with a dreaded "disease in his feet." Although he had been "fully committed to the Lord all of his life," it didn't occur to him to ask for help from God for his diseased feet. And because it's mentioned in the Bible, I can't help but think that irked God as well.

So, you see, we can do a lot to irk God and still get a final judgment of "fully committed" and "did what was good and right." This is not to say that we should. The point is that our God is merciful – He loves us with a perfect love that takes everything into account. He doesn't necessarily condemn us on the basis of one mistake, one false move or one huge botch. Likewise, we should not condemn others based on one huge botch.

We may be able to improve our justice system, but we can never have the perfect judgment that God has because we don't know it all. Whereas, for social control, we may find it necessary to impose penalties and restrict liberties to try to curb future infractions, we must resist the sinful and foolish temptation to judge a person's soul.

Who will have eternal life? Who will come through like a man rescued from the flames? Who will not be rescued from the flames? Who knows! Only God.

Hold this thought: Like I said, you can't judge a book by its cover.

I Wouldn't Touch it with a 10-Foot Pole

Drive out the mocker, and out goes strife; quarrels and insults are ended.

Proverbs 22:10

Do not make friends with a hot-tempered man, do not associate with one easily angered, or you may learn his ways and get yourself ensnared.

Proverbs 22:24

Can a person scoop hot coals into her lap without her clothes being burned?

Proverbs 6:27

We may be friendly people, but we don't want to be friends with everyone. Whereas we want to be kind to everyone, life is too short to become entangled with people who disturb our peace. Note that the proverb says "drive out" and "do not make friends with" and "do not associate with." Sounds a little harsh, but that is the essence of a message God conveys over and over in His word, and yes, even in the New Testament out of the mouth of Christ Himself. We are to separate ourselves from destructive people.

This was God's clear instruction to the Israelites when they took possession of the Promised Land: drive out all the others because of their impurity – not racial or ethnic impurity, but moral impurity. Christ told His disciples to shake from their feet the dust of the homes that wouldn't accept His message (Matthew 10:14). Discrimination, on the basis of moral purity, is actually Biblical. We are warned not to marry unbelievers and elsewhere reminded that though we are in this world, we're not to be a part of this world. As God's children, we are to preserve ourselves from the corrupting influences of the world, including violence, sexual immorality, greed, selfishness and all the songs, movies, books, magazines and people who represent these corrosive forces. Why? Are we elite? Well, we are the children of the King, but there is a much more practical rationale for separating ourselves from the world – it's called abundant life.

Jesus said, "I have come that they may have life and have it abundantly" (John 10:10). That's the whole point. God, our Father, and Jesus, our Big Brother, Advocate and Savior, want us to live and live well, in this life and the next. So they call us away from the things that lead to death and destructive living. And because there are some people in our paths who will not heed the call, we have to separate from them for our good.

151

Disease spreads; it's a law of the universe. We can't will an apple to stay fresh when it's sitting adjacent to a rotten apple. The law of nature is that the rot from the one will spread to the other. The only way to preserve that fresh apple is to pick it up and move it away from the rotted apple. And so it is with us, however much we'd like to think we're immune to "apple rot," the only way to preserve ourselves from it is to separate ourselves from it.

Many people today perceive this separation from the world as a penalty – "I have to give up…" whatever to be a Christian. That is really looking at the glass as half empty. The half-full version is to focus on the abundant life we have free from the world's sin. We get peace, security, true happiness! Nothing God asks us to walk away from is worth crying over – it's all garbage anyway, sometimes dressed in Abercrombie and looking so fine, but garbage nonetheless.

It's easy enough to resist porn flicks and lewd music and topless bars – who needs them? Satan creates that crap for the hopelessly reprobate – he doesn't even expect it to tempt us.

For us good girls, he has much more subtle temptations. In fact, he learned he couldn't get good girls to go see R-rated movies, so he fashioned something called PG-13. Satan knew we'd never pick up a porn magazine, so he created the fashion magazine that we can feel OK about buying and still have the opportunity to read about how to please a man six different ways with an egg beater. And Satan knew we'd never allow ourselves to get involved with an outright jerk, so he has chosen some very fly, smart and funny guys in which to infuse with anger, hatred and a violent temper, of which we'll be completely unaware until it literally smacks us across the face one day.

152

Don't be naïve. There's a universe-wide battle between Good and evil in progress as we speak and our soul is the prize. Though Good is so much more powerful (and we know Good prevails in the end), it seems sometimes that God is at a disadvantage on the battlefield. He has to play fair – it's His nature. Satan, on the other hand, can and does use all means of deception in his battle plan. And one of his most powerful plots is to use God's own word to deceive the people trying to please God.

God's word says, "Love one another." And so, in our efforts to stay on God's side of the battle, we can allow ourselves to become too involved/entangled/ensnared with a soul Satan has claimed. We may believe our involvement with that person is what's needed to bring him or her to God's side. And so we remain close to that person, despite their violence, hatred and sexual immorality. We try for a long time through a close relationship to be a good influence

> Satan knew we'd never pick up a porn magazine, so he created the fashion magazine that we can feel OK about buying and still have the opportunity to read about how to please a man six different ways with an egg beater.

on a person lost in sin. But what happens is that we eventually lose our focus on trying and then one day, we wake up and realize we're the ones that have been influenced – we've rotted!

I can just hear the desperate young woman cornered by this reasoning putting forth one last impenetrable defense: "That won't happen to me! I'm not you. I'm different, my circumstances are different and I can assure you that will not happen in my case."

I call this an impenetrable defense because it is not possible to prove this wrong in the present. Only time can bust through this last-ditch defense and when it does, and it inevitably does, it's too late – we've been proven wrong after the fact and we've lost a lot in the process.

153

Maybe we are different and maybe we are more rot-resistant than others. Maybe we do have super-human ability to hold hot coals in our lap and not get burned. Thousands of years of human experience argue to the contrary. Does betting on ourselves against wisdom gleaned from thousands of years of human experience seem like a good bet? If it does, we're either extremely mathematically challenged or we may have rotted already.

Hold this thought: I will keep myself physically separated from the sin of the world so it doesn't rub off on me.

Marked for Life

If you argue your case with a neighbor, do not betray another person's confidence, or she who hears it may shame you and you will never lose your bad reputation.

Proverbs 25:9-10

When I was a freshman in college, my workstudy job was in the financial aid office – an assignment I far preferred to something such as working in the cafeteria. I did light clerical work – mind-numbing stuff like filing, collating and stapling. To make my job more interesting, as I filed away confidential financial aid forms, I would take note of some juicy details of the files such as how much money the student's family made.

Upon my hiring, my boss, Fran Andrea, had told me that I would be around confidential information and that I was to keep it to myself – always. In general, I did, but there were also a couple of times that I used my knowledge to chime in about a certain student when he or she was the topic of conversation among my friends. I may have said, "Peter's family makes over $200,000 a year!" and other similar statements. I really can't say how many times I did this. It wasn't a lot, but even if it was only once, it was one time too many. Apparently, someone listening in had higher convictions on the issue of confidentiality than I did – so much so that they took action.

One day Fran Andrea pulled me aside and said she had received a report that I was disclosing confidential information. In one second, the blood drained from my head. The next, it all rushed back. I searched my memory frantically for the circumstances of any one time I had made such statements. I couldn't remember anything about any time – whom I had said it to, or about whom I had said it. Under her bright light of interrogation, I knew she was, in general, correct, but I didn't have any specifics. I told her I didn't know what she was talking about. I completely denied it and at the time, I distorted the truth to convince myself that the info I had leaked was not specific enough to be a breach of confidentiality.

Fran put me on probation. I worked that way for about two weeks more and then quit. I could not stomach going to work under the shroud of distrust. I felt like everyone in the office was watching me to see if my eyes lingered too long on any particular file. I developed conspiracy theories about another student who worked with me who wanted to get me fired so she could be the queen student bee in the financial aid office.

And outside of work, I suspected my friends. Which of them would have gone to Fran Andrea and told her such a thing – obviously the most scrupulous among them – but which one was it? I was angry and ashamed. Even though I didn't reveal to my friends my reason for quitting the financial aid office, I imagined the one who had gone to Fran Andrea had put two and two together and filled in all the rest of my friends. I imagined they all knew that I had resigned under suspicions of disclosing confidential information.

I don't know how much of that was real and how much was imagined, but I do know that I instantly felt like the whole world was thinking they couldn't trust me with secrets. I felt exposed as a big blabbermouth. It was humiliating.

As the days, weeks and months passed, the feelings of humiliation did too. On a day-to-day basis in my three remaining years of college, that dark memory didn't haunt me. But whenever I walked by the financial aid office (which fortunately was not really on the path to

> I instantly felt like the whole world was thinking they couldn't trust me with secrets. I felt exposed as a big blabbermouth.

anywhere), whenever I saw that other student who had worked in the office with me and whenever I heard the name or otherwise thought of Fran Andrea, that same sick feeling of knowing there were people out there who believed me to be untrustworthy would roll over me.

I never had too much more to do with Fran Andrea. I don't even remember if I ever saw her again, except across campus or in a crowd. I believe, though, that if we met again by chance tomorrow, as soon as she could place my name and face, the first thing on her mind would be, "that was the one who I disciplined for breach of confidentiality." That's what I'll always be to her.

Hold this thought: Tempting as it may be to share, I'll keep other people's secrets.

The Speed Trap

Those who forsake the law praise the wicked, but those who keep the law resist them.
If anyone turns a deaf ear to the law, even his prayers are detestable.

Proverbs 28:4, 9

The law these verses specifically referred to is Mosaic law; however, I believe these admonitions hold true for the laws of today as well. That takes a lot of faith for me to say because I have issues with the law. For starters, we have so many – federal, state, municipal – that it's impossible for any person to know them all and therefore, impossible for anyone to keep them all. Just as the Israelites found it impossible to comply to the letter of Mosaic law, it is impossible to live in complete compliance with the law today – even the ones we know about. Have you ever met a licensed driver who has never sped in her life? I doubt I have. What about those non-drivers? I bet every one of them has jaywalked at some point in their life.

Complete compliance with the law is social perfection and simply not within human grasp. That doesn't mean we need to give up on trying. To say, "I can't do it so why try," is a practical expression of forsaking the law. Do you see why it praises the wicked, as our proverb says? If we, as generally upstanding citizens, give up on trying to abide by the law, how can we expect people of lesser character and worse upbringing to try? It's as good as saying to them, "You're justified in your criminal acts because I can't keep myself from speeding either." It's absurd. For society to work, we have to have faith in the law – even if we do violate it because the person in line in front of us at Starbucks couldn't make up his mind and now we're running late to an important appointment!

If preserving the fabric of society isn't reason enough to keep the faith in the law, how about doing it to please God – or more accurately, to keep from becoming detestable in His sight. Do you see that in the verse above? Our prayers are detestable if we ignore the law. We're not talking about the occasional infraction that we regret as we're doing it and afterwards resolve to try harder in the future to avoid breaking the law. We're talking about a habitual disregard for the law – the kind of antisocial mental programming that plagues so many of us with constant thoughts of ways to get away with breaking the law, consequently pitting us against the authorities whose job it is to serve and protect.

158

Have you ever heard a parent tell her child, "You better stop that or the police will get you and put you in jail"? Or, "You have to wear your seat belt or the police will give you a ticket"? From very young, we are taught to comply with the law out of fear of the consequences.

In theory, the law is in place for the same reasons we have police, to serve and protect. Instead of recognizing the reason for the law – "You better put your seat belt on so you'll be safe in the car" – we use a negative motivation that transfers the reason to comply with the law away from how it benefits us and toward the fear of punishment. What we have as a result is a society that has a general disdain for the law and the public servants that enforce it. It's quite the opposite of how it should be.

I admit that it's hard to respect some laws because they are not in the spirit of the law. Some laws serve and protect special interest groups over the greater good of society. Other laws worked for a little while, but don't work anymore. We have too many old laws on the books that need to be stricken and too many new laws coming in all the time. Our system is overburdened. Our country is in desperate of need of some very creative legal reform that results in a legal system – from Congress to the courtroom – that is more simple and dynamic. Wouldn't it be great to have law that could actually be contained in one book and law that would be relevant and current within say a year or so of changing social forces? Instead, we have laws against selling used mattresses – vestiges from the days of corn husk mattresses; and my favorite – a recent law in Arkansas that allows children of any age to marry with their parents' consent. Apparently that was the result of a typo, but now legislators have to go through an involved process to amend the law, when common sense tells us it should not be legal to wed an infant.

159

No doubt, we have reason and even an obligation to seek to reform the laws of our land, but that does not excuse a disregard for the law as it is now. Recall that God puts kings on thrones. God is in control, even if we can't see a trace of it.

When we've been praying about an issue for a long time and are not seeing any resolution, perhaps it's time to take stock of our compliance with the law. Do we pirate music, movies or steal cable service? Do we plagiarize on term papers? Are we speeding to and fro, slowing down only for speed traps? Do we earn income, such as tips, that we're not reporting on our taxes? What kind of citizens are we?

Hold this thought: With God, there is no separation of church and state.

Good for the Soul

*She who conceals her sins does not prosper, but whoever confesses
and renounces them finds mercy.*

Proverbs 28:13

160

Do you have a dirty little secret? Maybe you've already repent-
ed and been forgiven of it and you wonder what is the point of
confessing it? Well, here's your answer. Concealing evil deeds
will keep us from prospering. And all the things we imagine
might happen if we confess the evil? That's just fear, brought
to us by Satan himself, to hold us back from prosperity. In this
verse, we see the promise of confession; it's mercy.

Confession is an integral part of the Catholic and Episcopalian
doctrines. Most Protestants reject the idea of confession to a
person in order to obtain God's forgiveness. True, God is the
one who forgives, but scripture does support confession to
another person – not just by prayers in our head (James 5:16).
However, that's rarely practiced in Protestant denominations.
Even a few decades ago, it was common for Protestants to at
least walk to the front of the congregation or the altar to accept
Christ, making a symbolic gesture of confession. Now it seems
that confession by mouth is a thing of the past. Wherever we
are standing or sitting, we can "just repeat this simple prayer"
to receive Christ into our hearts. Yes, that works and there's no
disputing it. Christ can be anywhere and bring us into the fold
even if we're incapable of uttering a word. However, in that process, there is no confession by mouth. And in more cases than
not, I fear people are just going about their business afterward
without ever actually telling someone, "I realized I was a sinner
and that I needed forgiveness."

Why is that so hard to say? We're ashamed of it, that's why.

And perhaps we're ashamed of what we've done to remedy it – of our decision to accept Christ. Consequently, those around us don't know where we stand. Friends and family may note some difference in our behavior and attitudes as we begin to grow spiritually, but they can't say for sure what the cause of the change is. "Maybe she's just maturing." We keep everyone guessing about the status of our soul.

That's not a very auspicious start to a life-time of service to God. We've just slipped into the ranks without being noticed, our eyes cast downward, hoping no one will point us out as being new to the Lord's army. Shame on us. Really, shame is on us when we do this. We are ashamed and shame on us for being ashamed.

Worse than shame though is how we cheat ourselves out of the blessing of prosperity. If I've described your situation and you have also happened to notice that this Christianity thing doesn't seem to be making a huge difference in your life, try this: Write a mass e-mail announcing that you are a Christian. Better yet, post it on your Facebook homepage or MySpace page. Who cares if it happened three years ago or when you were a kid. If you're an incognito Christian, come out of the closet now. Something simple will do: "God recently revealed to me the importance of confession. So I wanted to let every-one know that a few years ago, I realized I was a sinner in need of a Savior and I gave my life to Christ. I'm writing this because I think there may be some people who don't know this about me, and it's something you should really know about me."

I don't believe we need to confess the specific sin that made us realize we're sinners. The truth is there are a lot of different sins that make us sinners. Many of them we're unaware of until we come to know Christ and over time, God reveals them to us. However, I think there can be value in confessing specific sins, particularly if doing so will serve as a motivation for others to avoid making the same mistakes. This was my motivation in publishing online the journal I wrote to my deceased son. I always knew that sex outside of marriage was a sin, but reasoning it out, I figured the only one I was hurting was me. That was a trade off I was willing to make, especially since I lived in denial that my sin would ever catch up with me anyway. Well, it did. And that's what the journal is about. It's something young women are not being made aware of enough. I encourage you to read the journal; it's available online only as a free e-book download at www.OnMyOwnNow.com.

Hold this thought: I confess that I was lost in sin but am no more.

The Tapestry of Justice

Do not say, "I'll pay you back for this wrong!" Wait for the Lord, and he will deliver you.

Proverbs 20:22

Evil people do not understand justice, but those who seek the Lord understand it fully.

Proverbs 28:5

One of the very first values American parents try to teach their children is the concept of justice: "You can't take that toy away, he was playing with it." "Wait your turn." "Give Joey one and you can have one; that's fair." And so we grow up expecting that other things in life will be fair and then time and time again, we feel infuriated when we realize things aren't fair. We never stop wishing and wanting things to be fair like Mommy used to make them.

I often wonder why parents even bother trying to make things right. It's a cruel irony to teach children to play fair and then send them out into a world that doesn't. Seems it would be better preparation to teach children the difference between fair and unfair without trying to fix things all the time so they are fair – to use the injustices of play as opportunities to teach them to respond positively, to be undaunted by injustice.

We may be able to fix child's play, but we can't fix a teacher's bias in favor of the blue-eyed, fair-skinned child; we can't fix poverty; we can't fix child labor; we can't fix violence against women and the list goes on. If we dwell for very long on any one of the significant issues we can't fix, it becomes maddening. What can we do about the big injustices in the world if we can't even set things right when someone steals our parking spot?

We can totally relate to the prophet Jeremiah when he calls out to God, "Let me see your vengeance upon them!" (Jeremiah 20:12b). Because we're made in God's completely just image, a part of us yearns for justice. Left unchecked, our sinful nature can turn our God-like yearning for justice into a sinful desire for retaliation. God's will is not retaliation, but rather justice for all. Only a God who is all good can mete out justice, and speaking for myself, I'm sure glad God's justice is inextricably fused with compassion and love for each of us.

But why can't we help God along a bit to bring about justice? The fundamental problem with us trying to "help" God's will to be done in these matters is that we don't know the whole story. What seems like a just solution to us may actually be an even worse injustice than we're reacting to in the first place.

In the face of life's monumental and mundane injustices, our proverb advises against trying to even the score. So if we shouldn't say, "I'll get you for this!" can we say, "You'll get yours!"? However true that may be, that desperate prophecy bears the same sentiment as "I'll get you for this!" The difference is an understanding and acceptance of the fact that we won't be the one dishing out the justice. That is a more informed retort, but still comes from an attitude of wanting to retaliate.

What does our proverb say will happen if we will forbear in the face of injustice? Wait and the Lord will…rain fire and brimstone on our enemy? No, the Lord will deliver us! And what are we being delivered from? Well, presumably from the injustice, but I happen to know firsthand, that when we wait on the Lord, He also delivers us from the rage we feel as a result of the injustice and our natural desire to see punishment heaped out on the one who did us wrong. When we call on God to work in a situation, God will deliver us to a full understanding of justice.

A few generations ago, my family started a non-profit organization that was managed for a time in the 1990s by a distant cousin of mine. When my sister took over administration in the early 2000s, she discovered that money was missing – and a lot of it! She involved me and together we uncovered that our cousin had cashed out company CDs without the permission or knowledge of the directors. He had used that money for purchasing a new Suburban and had invested the rest in a stock that soon went belly-up when the market crashed after September 11, 2001. The more we dug, the more we found and soon we had enough evidence to put our cousin away for a few years in jail. We sought the council of the FBI and they told us that if the current directors were in agreement with prosecuting, they would file the case with the federal prosecutor.

165

The directors consisted of other family members and some friends of the family. Not all were in agreement with prosecuting. Though all agreed he had done wrong (the evidence was indisputable), they thought that perhaps they should show him mercy.

During the months this unraveled, we communicated many times with our cousin. He started out in denial but when we presented the evidence to him, his response became similar to that of a cornered animal. Instead of repenting for his actions, he tried to justify them and counterattacked with insults to mine, my sister's and my mother's character. Though his accusations were false and unfounded, they confused the situation, as lies tend to do. Our entire family was in turmoil – some being sure of the truth and others doubting it, even with objective

I asked God to make it all straight and I meant that I wanted, at a minimum, to see my cousin appear repentant and perhaps even be caught in some other deception in which there would be no family members to have mercy on him.

proof in front of them.

"Upset," "mad" and even "distraught" do not begin to describe what my sister, mother and I felt during that time. We wanted "justice" but other key stakeholders didn't feel that way. No charges were ever made. The directors did disassociate him from the organization with the caveat that if he ever wanted anything to do with the organization in the future, his first step would be to pay back the money he had stolen. That didn't seem sufficient to me. I prayed that God would intervene. I asked God to make it all straight and I meant that I wanted, at a minimum, to see my cousin appear repentant and perhaps even be caught in some other deception in which there would be no family members to have mercy on him. The cherry on top of this whole thing is that he was, and still is, a pastor of a church. It was all so very wrong!

As is often true, I had no choice but to wait for the Lord because there was nothing I could do. And so I waited and waited for months and years. As I waited, the Lord began to work. And if you reread our proverb, you'll know what the Lord did. The Lord delivered me! I have no idea what happened to my cousin, but now it doesn't matter. I have forgiven him (to be more accurate, I am forgiving him) and I am delivered from all the anger and resentment generated by the injustice. I have accepted that God is in control of that situation and God will have justice.

I have a favorite poem called "The Weaver" by Grant Colfax Tuller. I'm going to paraphrase a part of it here:

Life is one great tapestry between my God and me.
I cannot choose the colors that He works on steadily.
Often I don't like the colors He chooses, but in my
 foolish pride,
I've forgotten God sees the upper, and I the underside.

Have you ever seen the underside of a tapestry or an embroidery? It's a mess and well, ugly! But when you turn it around to the top, you see how, from a different perspective, those same mangled threads of the underside create perfection on the top. Our perspective on all things in this life and from this earth is like looking at the back of the tapestry. We simply cannot see how it all fits together until we're on the other side, that is, when we pass from this life to the next. Such is our perspective on justice. All our unanswered questions that leave us feeling desperate and full of rage will be explained when we see the view from above.

In the meantime, on this side of the tapestry, in order to maintain our sanity in the face of the world's many injustices, we must trust that the Great Weaver is creating perfection, though it's not obvious to us. This is the full understanding we are promised.

Hold this thought: Heavenly Father, deliver me from my unproductive, negative feelings caused by injustice.

chapter six

To Befriend and Be a Friend

She Got Game

I'll Take Door #1

The Truth, the Whole Truth and Nothing but the Truth, so Help me God

Maybe a Rock, But NOT an Island

Tears of Joy and Other Paradoxes

SOS

She Got Game

She who walks with the wise grows wise, but a companion of fools suffers harm.

Proverbs 13:20

I love to play volleyball but I don't do it that often. It's not so hard to find an impromptu game of volleyball to join – almost anything can serve as a net and you don't have to have an official volleyball either, even beach balls work for the basic game. However, I'm very finicky about with whom I play volleyball. 169 From my experience, if I join a game in which people are slapping at the ball every which way – a variation I call jungle ball – I find I cannot play well. What good does the perfect bump into the front center do if there is no one to set the ball? What's the use of trying to set when you have no one to spike? Try as I might, I end up playing jungle ball too and that frustrates me.

On the other hand, when I join a game of serious players I find that my skills sharpen and if I'm the worst player on the court, I play an excellent game, for me, because I am trying so hard not to embarrass myself!

When I play volleyball, I unintentionally rise or fall to the level of the players around me. In jungle ball, my game goes bad. With some serious players, I got game.

This chameleon-like phenomenon is not at play just in sports. It works with our minds, our senses of humor, our ethics, our levels of racial prejudice or tolerance and our spirituality, among many other things. We'd like to think that as independent, self-contained units, our peers, teammates and colleagues can't bring us down. Not so. We have to work at keeping all our games good – those of mind, body and soul – and the people we choose to "play" with have a big impact on which way our game goes.

Maybe we have a group of friends who practice some behavior that we don't, but we like hanging out with them and they seem to respect that fact that we don't do said behavior. The relationship works. We get the best of them and they don't get the best of us – so we think. We may never start doing the thing they do that we don't, but at very least, we're learning a tolerance for their behavior and we're learning that we can really like a person who does "such and such" and that simple change in us can have a profound influence on us and bring our game down.

170   I had a friend who smoked. She and I decided to move in together to lower our expenses. She never pressured me to smoke and was very courteous about not smoking inside the house. I found I could tolerate her smoking with good manners quite well. That arrangement only lasted a few months. We moved on to other housing arrangements having forged a lasting friendship as a result of our cohabitating. It's all good, right?

Less than a year later, I met a nice-looking guy at work and started to grow fond of him. Then I found out he smoked. In general, I did not like the thought of dating a smoker. I think it's a self-destructive and nasty habit! Yet, because of my experience with my courteous smoker friend, the idea of dating a smoker did not have the shock value for me that it used to. I knew from experience that I could live with a smoker.

I started dating "the smoker" and though I knew early on the relationship was not going to work in the long term, it took three years to run its course. That was three years of breathing second-hand smoke and enduring kissing a smoker and all that goes with being a nonsmoker dating a smoker.

I started dating "the smoker" and though I knew early on the relationship was not going to work in the long term, it took three years to run its course. That was three years of breathing second-hand smoke and enduring kissing a smoker and all that goes with being a nonsmoker dating a smoker. Those were three hard years of relationship for many reasons, smoking being the least of them. In the final analysis, I would have been better off never having dated "the smoker." I wonder if I had not had that fairly neutral experience with a smoking housemate, if I would have been turned off by that nice-looking guy's detestable habit and spared myself the major heartache that was that wasted three years of relationship.

The point is that hanging with people we do *not* wish to become like will pull us in directions we do not wish to go. If we have a vision of the kind of person we want to be – or we like the kind of person we are – then we should surround ourselves with people that match that vision. It's not being a snob to select our friends carefully. Be kind to everyone, but when it comes to rubbing shoulders, remember that people rub off. So rub up next to someone who's got the game you want.

Hold this thought: I hang with people whose character I admire.

I'll Take Door #1

Wisdom has built her house; she has hewn out its seven pillars. She has prepared her meat and mixed her wine; she has also set her table. She has sent out her maids, and she calls from the highest point of the city. **"Let all who are simple come in here!" she says to those who lack judgment.** *"Come, eat my food and drink the wine I have mixed. Leave your simple ways and you will live; walk in the way of understanding. … For through me your days will be many, and years will be added to your life."*

Proverbs 9:1-6, 11

The woman Folly is loud; she is undisciplined and without knowledge. She sits at the door of her house, on a seat at the highest point of the city, calling out to those who pass by, who go straight on their way. **"Let all who are simple come in here!" she says to those who lack judgment.** *"Stolen water is sweet; food eaten in secret is delicious!" But little do they know that the dead are there, that her guests are in the depths of the grave.*

Proverbs 9:13-18

If you are wise, your wisdom will reward you.

Proverbs 9:12a

Let's do a little compare and contrast. Here are two recruiters who want to attract simple people to their way. Both strategically position themselves at the highest point in the city, wait for someone lacking in judgment to come along, and then, both call out – maybe at the exact same time, "Let all who are simple come in here!"

Double-take! What's a simpleton to do – two identical invitations from two attractive women? Stunned by indecision, he listens as each offers more selling points.

Wisdom says, "Come, eat my food and drink the wine I have mixed. Leave your simple ways and you will live; walk in the way of understanding."

"Eh, sounds OK," thinks the simpleton.

Folly counters, "Stolen water is sweet; food eaten in secret is delicious."

"Now that's what I'm talking about!" shouts the simpleton.

Both Wisdom and Folly offered food and drink, but Folly has made an excitement-based appeal. Walking in the way of understanding quite frankly sounds boring compared to stealthy epicurean adventures and sneaking stolen water. Nonetheless, from our vantage point, it seems obvious which woman's invitation the simpleton should accept.

"Go with Wisdom, you fool!" the audience yells.

However, in real-life scenarios, when we're the one the women are calling out to, it's not so cut and dried – knowing which invitation to accept is not quite as easy. Maybe this sounds familiar: one friend invites us to go to her house on the lake over the weekend and another invites us to a rock concert.

One says, "Come have dinner at my house and meet my family," and another says, "Double with me with two guys I met last night."

One invites us to go to a church cookout and another invites us to girls' night out.

These choices are much harder. In our heart and head, we know the safe choice is the lake, the family dinner, the cookout, but the prospect of the concert, double date and girls' night out stir up some adrenaline. C'mon, unless you're a huge fan of barbeque, who wouldn't rather go out with the girls? It just sounds like more fun!

We rationalize our choice: one night won't make or break us; we don't want to seem rude; we'll do it just this once to build rapport but we won't make a habit of it; we've wanted a chance

173

to witness to this person; blah, blah, blah...

In Solomon's scenario, Wisdom's and Folly's invitations are just for dinner. But in reality, the choice before us at each invitation is the choice between wisdom and folly, the choice between two ways of life: abundant life or slow death.

Ironically, choosing wisdom and life requires some self-denial. It doesn't feel like abundant life to accept the dinner invitation and watch the double date go to another friend. It doesn't feel like abundant life the next day when we hear how awesome the concert was, how gorgeous the dates were, the hilariously bizarre things that happened on girls' night out, and we, in turn, can say of our evening only that, "It was nice."

174

On behalf of life in general and the laws of the universe, I apologize that what is good for us often does not *feel* good. Sincerely, I am sorry, for both you and me. Just like broccoli going down, an immunization going in, and muscles building up, those things that will make us stronger and live longer often require mental discipline to accept. Further, I am terribly sorry that so many things that feel good are actually very bad for us. One of life's great paradoxes (of which there are many): Folly feels good right now and punishes later. Wisdom requires self-denial but rewards greatly later.

For making wise choices, our rewards will be peace, joy and long life. Not feeling it? Try thinking of someone you know whose life is a total wreck. If you're at a complete loss to pinpoint one of your own acquaintances who qualifies, tune into a sensationalist talk show. Let your thoughts dwell on the life of this total wreck just

> On behalf of life in general and the laws of the universe, I apologize that what is good for us often does not feel good. Sincerely, I am sorry, for both you and me.

until your head begins to involuntarily wag in dismay. Would you trade the peace of your life for the daily mayhem of that unfortunate soul? Now you're feeling it. Peace, joy and long life rock!

Gaining the peace and joy of a wise life are well worth the small sacrifice we will make for them. And on the bright side, there could be some cute guys at that church cookout!

Hold this thought: Every choice matters.

175

The Truth, the Whole Truth and Nothing but the Truth, so Help me God

The first to present her case seems right till another comes forward and questions her.

Proverbs 18:17

The singular story I remember from Sunday school about King Solomon is about the time he suggested splitting the baby in half to resolve a dispute between two women. Do you remember this story? Two women who live together, both mothers of newborns, come before Solomon. One of the babies has died and the grieving mother is now claiming the living child. It's one woman's word against the other. There are no witnesses. Both are convincing – one has the sincere emotion of a mother fighting to keep her baby; the other is charged with the emotion of grief over the loss of her own baby.

The argument heats up and Solomon swiftly orders the infant in question seized and split in half. He tells the women they can each have half. Both women react from the gut, the mother with urgency to save the child, and the other, out of the anger of grief, enthusiastically agrees to the solution. She would rather no one have a baby than for her alone to be denied a child. Unwittingly, she reveals herself. This case helped earn Solomon the lasting reputation of being a very wise and discerning judge.

It's interesting to see what the greatest judge in human history has to say in the verse above. I think most people would say they could spot a lie when confronted with one. And some lies are apparent. However, particularly in disputes in which there may be some fault on both sides, it is extremely difficult to sort out the truth. Solomon says the first one seems right. Then when the next one speaks, she seems right. The next verse tells us how Solomon resolved a lot of these cases in which both sides had strong arguments and neither would admit fault: "Casting the lot settles disputes." Yes, the greatest judge the world has known resorted to a coin toss on many occasions in which he couldn't figure out on which side the truth lay.

I have seen the truth of this proverb on many occasions in my position as a court-certified mediator. After about a year of mediating civil cases, I specialized in divorce cases. I learned very quickly not to draw any conclusions based on the opening remarks of the plaintiffs, because as soon as it was the defendant's turn to talk, an entirely different light was cast on the story. A mediator's job is not to decide matters but to facilitate the two parties at arriving at a self-crafted resolution. I'm so glad I didn't have to decide who was right. I often spent several hours working through issues with a couple, and when it was all over, I still had no idea who was telling the truth and who was lying.

The reason it's so difficult to settle a dispute like that is because seldom is either party completely innocent. In the vast majority of disputes, from divorces to the petty arguments that keep friends from talking to each other, both sides have been wronged and both sides are at fault. This is a hard truth for Americans to wrap their minds around. We are raised believing in the dichotomy of right and wrong. That does exist, but mostly on moral issues. In the more mundane issues of everyday stress and strife, humans will be human and that usually means we mess up – all of us. And so, whose fault is it that you and your boyfriend are fighting? Whose fault is it when your best friend won't speak to you for two days? Whose fault is it that you haven't spoken to your parents in months? It's some theirs and some yours.

I haven't talked to my father in years. The last conversation I had with him, I was inviting him to my wedding and explaining at the same time why I was specifically not inviting his wife and their children. My case is long; suffice to say, I was justified in not wanting her there and even my father said, "I don't blame you." I do regret not having invited the children though.

My father lived about three hours from where my wedding was to take place. However, on my wedding day, he happened to be only a 30-minute drive from the church just before the wedding, but he didn't come. He didn't call. He didn't send a card with his brother or sisters who all attended. And that was the beginning of the silence between us.

If I had to go before a judge, mediator or arbiter, I could make an extremely convincing case for his fault in why we no longer speak. The crowning point in my argument would be that even when my son died, he did not call or send a card, let alone attend the funeral of his only grandson. Yet I know in my heart that I had a large role in the rift, too. I may have been justified in what I did, but my specific action – a refusal to invite his wife to my wedding – brought years of tolerable antipathy to a head. Yes, I did something to cause the rift.

When God finally got that message through to me, I wrote my father an apology for my part in our silence. That was some time ago and though nothing has changed between my father and me, there is a big difference – I've asked for forgiveness for my role in the dispute.

There are two truths I want you to hold on to from this verse – the first one for when you find yourself as the neutral third party in the middle of a cat fight, the other for when you're one of the cats.

Hold these thoughts:
I can help resolve problems without choosing sides.
When there's trouble, I may be part of the problem.

Maybe a Rock, But NOT an Island

A woman's spirit sustains her in sickness, but a crushed spirit, who can bear?

Proverbs 18:14

The news of a suicide and even attempted suicide almost always gives me pause to consider the emotional state of the person who took his or her own life. It's a low, low place where one decides that to die under a curse is better than to live another day. Rarely is this a place to which a person comes quickly. There are events so devastating that they instantly can turn essentially happy people into candidates for suicide – utter public humiliation or the death of an intimate friend or family member, for example. However, most often, if we contemplate the life of the person who committed suicide, we see a slow deterioration, a long period of desperation and a gradual conclusion that life will not improve. The backdrop of these grim circumstances could be a chemical imbalance that causes depression, mania or both.

I believe many chemical imbalances may be a result of modern lifestyles but, praise God, modern medicine has kept pace and has the remedy to correct many chemical imbalances – if we're not too proud to seek help. A very basic solution to chemical imbalance is forming good habits of eating, sleeping and exercising: going to bed at the same hour every night, getting seven or eight hours of sleep, waking up to some exercise followed by a good breakfast and eating nutritious food at every meal (and no junk in between).

If 21 days of that routine doesn't brighten our outlook, the next thing short of medical intervention is to take a fistful of nutritional supplements each day. Start with a multivitamin and some St. John's wort*. Then ask a pharmacist to recommend some more supplements – explaining that we feel list-less and depressed. Or do a Google search on "nutritional supplements for depression," and see what comes up. Supplements are chemicals that change our body's chemistry and it is possible to correct a slight imbalance by taking them. If we try this and it works, don't stop taking them! We might try weaning ourselves from St. John's wort, but the vitamins are something our body needs every day for the rest of our lives.

Sadly, many people who have found relief by using supplements and pharmaceuticals stop taking them after they begin to feel better. Gradually, they start to feel bad again and it may not occur to them to return to what worked before. If supplements make us feel better, we've found the something our bodies were missing, so don't stop taking it! It's a small price to pay for an optimistic outlook.

Some people would rather see a doctor and take medicine for their problem or may have an imbalance so severe that medicine is the only solution. If that describes you, that's okay, just do it! When you feel depressed, you don't have to go to a psychiatrist for therapy. Believing a psychiatrist is the first stop may be keeping a lot of people from seeking medical help for depression because they aren't ready to go to that extreme. A regular medical doctor (primary care physician) can evaluate and treat the blues. Our lives are worth a visit to the doctor! Unfortunately, many people will let themselves sink past the point at which they can seek intervention into a despair so deep they are not capable of reaching out to anyone. And this is what I want you to be aware of and vigilant to not let happen to you!

There is always someone we can reach out to. Even many rural communities have suicide hotlines! They are a safety net for people who can't find a live person to talk to. If you begin to think of taking your life, your best bet is to involve a caring adult who you can talk to face-to-face. Go first to the person who loves you most. If you can't think of even one person who loves you, crack the yellow pages and turn to "churches." Start calling and take the first appointment you can get with either a youth minister or a pastor. Odds are very good that person loves you and you don't even know it yet. If you already go to a church and yet you still couldn't think of a single person who loves you, switch churches!

"A crushed spirit, *who can bear*?" says the proverb. Do you see the point? This is something we can't get through on our own. Reach out for help. First to heaven with a simple prayer, "Father, please lead me to the right help." Then reach out to someone or something on earth.

You know the song "Lean on Me," that says, "We all need somebody to lean on." That's so true. You don't have to feel one iota of shame about needing someone. We'd be freaks if we didn't ever need anyone. Needing others is a defining characteristic of our humanity. There is no shame in it, in fact, we can be proud of ourselves for being so sensible as to get help.

Hold this thought: I will find help when I need it.

*St. John's wort can interact poorly with some medications. If you take prescription medication, it is important to inform your healthcare provider about any herb or dietary supplement you would like to add, including St. John's wort, to ensure safe and coordinated care. See more at National Institutes of Health Web site, http://nccam.nih.gov/health/stjohnswort.

Tears of Joy and Other Paradoxes

Each heart knows its own bitterness and no one else can share its joy.

Proverbs 14:10

Even in laughter the heart may ache, and joy may end in grief.

Proverbs 14:13

Everyone who lives into adulthood knows deep, personal pain – an unreturned love, a forbidden love, a love stolen by death, the humiliation of failure, betrayal or rejection. These deep wounds in our soul at best only scar and though we can get to a point where they no longer hurt to think casually about them, if we start to probe and pick at that old wound, we find, under the scar tissue, it still hurts.

And yet we go on with life acting as if we don't hurt. Is that hypocrisy? No, it's complexity. God has made us both physically and emotionally very complex beings – able to simultaneously live successfully embracing both conflicting and seemingly irreconcilable feelings. In great sorrow we can laugh, and conversely, even in good company with much laughter, we can feel hauntingly alone.

Just before my daughter's sixth birthday, I received a call from her grandfather, giving me the news that her father had died in car accident. In turn, I had to pass this message on to my daughter – a dreaded responsibility. She began to cry as soon as the words came from my mouth. And we had a good cry. When the tears finally dried, I didn't know what to do next. It seemed irreverent to be concerned about such mundane things as what to have for breakfast, and yet life has to go on even for those who hurt.

It occurred to me to tell her that even though she was sad

and nothing could change that, it was okay if she wanted to play and have fun and run around and laugh. She could do all that and still be sad. And she did. Coincidentally, we had company that same morning and so she ran off to play with her company. Over the next weeks and months, her usual demeanor was little changed; she was the cheerful, fun-loving kid of always. But every now and then, she would come up to me, look up at me pathetically and say, "Daddy." I would say, "I know," and give her a hug and then she'd run off again to frolic and play some more.

I learned a lot from how she handled grief – mainly the truth 183
of what I inadvertently told her that morning – that we can be filled with grief and it is nonetheless okay to laugh and go about our business. Life is just that way. It doesn't stand still for heartache. Though if we could, we would certainly stop it and make everyone in the world acknowledge what a hard thing we have known and try to comfort us. Of course, we can't do that and even if we could, it wouldn't help.

Even if we are fortunate enough to have someone who is willing to take on the hurt, we simply cannot share it. No person can take your pain or even know your pain – even if he knows a similar pain of his own. When our baby, Hunter, died, my husband and I were equally grieved – both so heartbroken. But we couldn't feel each other's pain. We only felt our own pain and it was different from the other's pain. We responded differently – taking turns holding it together and losing it. The best we could do for each other was to hold hands, put arms around each other and think thoughts and prayers of comfort. We were together, in pain, yet alone in our pain.

> In great sorrow we can laugh, and conversely, even in good company with much laughter, we can feel hauntingly alone.

There is only one cure for a breaking heart and that is the balm from heaven. Ask God to pour out a healing balm to soothe your heart. When you really want relief from your pain, God will indeed give it to you. Asking for God's healing balm for my heart helped me get up and work and take care of my family on many days after Hunter died. If you will only believe as you ask, you will instantly feel the effects.

Hold this thought: Only God can cure my heartache.

184

SOS

Rescue those being led away to death; hold back those stagger-
ing toward slaughter. If you say, "But we knew nothing about this,"
does not he who weighs the heart perceive it? Does not he who
guards your life know it? Will he not repay each person according
to what she has done?

Proverbs 24:11-12

She who rebukes another will in the end gain more favor than she
who has a flattering tongue.

Proverbs 28:23

The last time I was in Los Angeles, I saw a crazy woman on a
street corner. She was dressed in a suit, and if she had cleaned
up just the slightest bit, she could have walked into a nearby
office building and fit in well. In physical appearance alone, she
didn't look crazy, but she was sure acting crazy. She was carrying on her own personal pantomime which I would entitle
"Cursing out the Devil." Slow traffic gave us the opportunity
to see her in action for a few minutes. She was scary! And yet
people walked by her on the sidewalk without even turning
their heads – treating her as if what she was doing was normal
(which indeed it may be for any given corner in Los Angeles!).

Clearly the woman needed help and a more sane response to
her would have been to call the men in white coats. Of course,
our mental health systems, particularly for people of low to
no income, are so overburdened that even if called, no men in
white coats would come to her aid. She's crazy and out of luck,
as are many of the people with mental illness on street corners
around the country. There's not much I can do to really help
someone like that – besides giving temporary relief in the form

of food or a hot cup of coffee.

Most of us know someone who has gone off the deep end – either clinically mentally ill or, undiagnosed, is just totally screwing up her life. We may call her "crazy." But you know what's really crazy? The fact that we respond to her as if she were completely sane!

Dysfunctional people don't spontaneously generate – they are formed through years of dysfunctional childhood. To turn a dysfunctional person into a functional, contributing member of society who isn't wrecking her own life requires more than some good advice and a hot meal. It requires years of relearning new, functional ways of living, if not some medication.

I have very little tolerance for religious people who think that accepting Jesus as Savior means that a person will wake up the next morning devoid of dysfunction. The Apostle Paul said (II Corinthians. 5:17), "Therefore, if anyone is in Christ, he is a new creation; the old has gone, the new has come!" But this was something even he could say only after spending three years recreating himself. Here's his story as he himself tells it (Galatians 1:13, 15-18, 22-24): "You have heard of my previous way of life in Judaism, how intensely I persecuted the church of God and tried to destroy it. But when God, who set me apart from birth and called me by his grace, was pleased to reveal his Son in me so that I might preach him among the Gentiles, I did not consult any man, nor did I go up to Jerusalem to see those who were apostles before I was, but I went immediately into Arabia and later returned to Damascus. Then after three years, I went up to Jerusalem to get acquainted with Peter and stayed with him fifteen days. I was personally unknown to the churches of Judea that are in Christ. They only heard the report, 'The man who formerly persecuted us is now preaching the faith he once tried to destroy.' And they praised God because of me."

People point to the Apostle Paul as a leopard who changed

his spots – he went from persecuting the early Christians to their greatest proponent. And though from one moment to the next, he was blind and then he saw the light (literally), we overlook the fact that he spent three years to become a new creature in Christ – being transformed by the renewing of his mind – to use his own words. Salvation by grace happens in a moment, but becoming a new creature takes a lot of work.

Somewhere along the road to Damascus for all of us, we need a kind of intervention that Saul (Paul) had. We need to see the light and hear some straight talk. And that's what's missing for many people today. If we know someone who needs to change, the worst thing we can do for that person is to respond to her as if she's making sense. When she says something crazy, if we really love her and want to help her, we should tell her she's not making sense. Tell her the thinking she's using is not going to achieve her desired outcome, and show her another way.

Are you catering to the dysfunction of someone you know and love? Are you reinforcing her errant walk by treating her as if she were making sense? Perhaps God has placed you in her life to be an agent of reality – to rescue this person who is ruining her life with foolish thinking and behavior. Pray up, then start talking straight.

Hold this thought: Out of love, I refuse to respond to dysfunction as if it were normal.

187

The Greatest of These is Charity

Quid Pro Quo

From Rags to Riches in Just 20 Years!

I Tithed out of Desperation

There's Always Something to Give

Quid Pro Quo

Honor the Lord with your wealth, with the firstfruits of your crops; then your barns will be filled to overflowing, and your vats will brim over with new wine. My daughter, do not despise the Lord's discipline and do not resent his rebuke, because the Lord disciplines those he loves, as a father the daughter he delights in. Blessed is the woman who finds wisdom, the woman who gains understanding, for wisdom is more profitable than silver and yields better returns than gold. Wisdom is more precious than rubies and nothing you desire can compare with her. Long life is in her right hand; in her left hand are riches and honor. Her ways are pleasant ways, and all her paths are peace. She is a tree of life to those who embrace her; those who lay hold of her will be blessed.

189

Proverbs 3:9-18

As a sort of "thank you" for all God gives, God asks us to honor Him by helping others. From every dollar that comes through our door, God wants us to take one dime and give it back to Him. Make someone else's life better with that first dime of every dollar. God promises that in return for our giving we will always have, not just enough, but all we need and some left over.

Read the proverb above one more time. Notice this sentence: "My daughter, do not despise the Lord's discipline and do not resent his rebuke, because the Lord disciplines those he loves, as a father the daughter he delights in." It's interjected in the middle of this passage about money. I wondered why that is. It almost seems like a sudden change of subject.

I offer the following paraphrase of our proverb which helped me to understand that the sudden remark about discipline actually is on-topic: "Give me back some of what I just gave you and you'll be glad you did. Don't hate me because I'm making this rule. I'm doing it for your own good. This is wise and if you'll do it, you'll end up with something more valuable than money, something you'll get a lot more out of than even gold."

God understands that giving away money we just worked so hard to earn is a tough one for us – it's where our spiritual, intangible faith becomes physical and, seemingly, a real sacrifice is required of us. God knows we won't take this lightly and are likely to be a little upset with Him about this principle – so He says, "Don't hate me for being a good father." What our Heavenly Father knows that we don't is how good for us our giving will eventually be.

If we are struggling with finances, what we need most is to give some money back to God. This sounds illogical, but it is another of the great paradoxical truths in life. Jesus said, "Give, and it will be given to you. A good measure, pressed down, shaken together and running over, will be poured into your lap. For with the measure you use, it will be measured to you" (Luke 6:38).

Dr. Robert Schuller calls this "the law of proportionate returns" – the more we give, the more we get. Yes, we'll get a lot of spiritual benefits, but God is promising here that we will have physical blessings too – money in savings (barns filled to overflowing) and the small luxuries we enjoy (vats brimming over with new wine).

> God knows we won't take this lightly and are likely to be a little upset with Him about this principle – so He says, "Don't hate me for being a good father."

In our excitement about being physically blessed, note this proverb also reminds us that understanding and wisdom benefit us far more than money, and through them, we can have riches, honor and a peaceful life – the things that society wants us to believe money can buy. We know from so many examples of rich, famous and yet completely miserable people, that money is not the source of satisfaction, peace and long life. Silver, gold and rubies can't buy self-esteem, love or peace of mind. These true treasures of life are free and available to anyone who finds wisdom and gets understanding.

Hold this thought: I give 10 percent of all my income to help other people.

From Rags to Riches in Just 20 Years!

A poor person pleads for mercy, but a rich woman answers harshly.

Proverbs 18:23

Were you born into a family that doesn't have to worry about money? If so, lucky you! If not, join the club.

192 Most of us can relate to having wanted something we or our parents could not afford. And you know what? That's a good thing. Maybe we only ever had that experience once or maybe we've known it almost every day of our lives. Regardless of how rare or frequent, it's not wasted experience. We can use the feelings that being denied stirs in us to create compassion for the poor.

Some people think they have a solution for the poor: "If they would only…" or, "If the president and Congress would only…" The fact of the matter is that poverty is one of the most complicated issues with which humanity has to deal. The solution is overly simple – poor people need money. The process is so complex that no society in all of human history has figured it out. Jesus said, "The poor you will always have with you" (Matthew 26:11). That says to me that some of us have to fulfill the role of being "the poor." Just don't let it be me, right?

Well, it has been me. My entire childhood, through college and the Peace Corps, I played the part of the "the poor." Starting with my first job after I returned from the Peace Corps, I switched roles and now play "the middle class," except for a brief period when I voluntarily returned to poverty to be able to take care of my grandparents in their old age and begin homeschooling my daughter. So, I know a little something about poverty. I could tell you how I got out, but it's no guaranteed-to-work-for-you solution.

The one thing from my experience that I believe does hold true for everyone is that if we are poor, it doesn't mean we always will be poor. This is particularly true for college students. Statistically, they've got a great chance of being middle class or better, even if they come from a poor family.

Going from poor to rich is a common transition in our society. We still call it "the American dream," but it happens so frequently that Americans have adopted a cultural view that anyone can pull herself up by her boot straps if she really has the desire to do it. If we've ever racked up a big credit card debt then tried to pay it off, or if we've ever tried saving for a down payment on a car, we know firsthand that bettering ourselves financially is not as easy as pulling on boot straps (whatever those are!).

193

With few exceptions, people who have shifted classes in their lifetimes don't do it instantly. We can't just wake up one day and say, "That's it! I've had it with being poor. Starting today I'm shifting classes and I will have completed my transition by this time tomorrow." That's ridiculous, of course, but my point is that bringing oneself out of poverty is most often a five-year, 10-year or even a 20- or 30-year plan. Even the great positive thinkers of the 20th century, like Zig Ziglar, started out with nothing and stayed that way a long time. Read the biographies and memoirs of famous people – athletes and entertainers included – most of these people struggled for decades with having enough money to pay the rent before their efforts finally paid off. Those hard luck stories are what makes their lives interesting and their books sell!

Are you living in lean years? Take comfort in knowing that you can improve your situation – you're in the best country in the world for class mobility – but it won't come quickly. You've got to pace yourself. Live within your means – meaning don't spend money you don't have. You can do without the laptop, cell phone and $70 Abercrombie T-shirt. Instead of watching television in your downtime, which is programmed intentionally to stir consumer desire within you, encourage yourself by reading life stories about people who made it out of poverty – there are so many. You can find their stories in magazines and books available for free at your local library – a fascinating place. Hang out with people who have gone through what you're going through. Talk to your parents, aunts, uncles and people at church about how they struggled. Adopt the attitude that you're in a long transition. You're not poor, you're becoming rich – it's just going to take some time.

194   We may want to get out of our situation as quickly as possible, but it will serve us in life. Learn to appreciate this experience – while we're still in it – for the perspective it will give us and the compassion for the poor it will create in us. If we come out of our poverty with the attitude, "I did it, why can't they?" we haven't learned the lesson of poverty. Poverty is discouraging; it colors our outlook everyday of the year; it limits our opportunity. When we make it out, we should thank God for giving us the necessary intelligence and skills and opportunities to capitalize on them. And when God gives us the opportunity to show compassion to a poor person, we must seize that in thanks to God that we're no longer poor (or that we never were).

Hold this thought: A poor person's life is hard enough without me adding to her grief. I can relate.

There's Always Something to Give

The wealth of the rich is their fortified city, but poverty is the ruin of the poor.

Proverbs 10:15

A poor person's field may produce abundant food, but injustice sweeps it away.

Proverbs 13:23

The poor are shunned even by their neighbors, but the rich have many friends.
She who despises her neighbor sins, but blessed is she who is kind to the needy.

Proverbs 14:20-21

She who oppresses the poor shows contempt for their Maker, but whoever is kind to the needy honors God.

Proverbs 14:31

As long as there are wealthy people, there will be poor people. Recall that Jesus said there will always be poor people. A child born into poverty and raised in poverty is not responsible for her poverty any more than she is responsible for being female. A life of disadvantage generally does not endow a person with skills and resources needed to bring oneself out of poverty. Yet some manage by hard work and blessing to escape poverty. There are even an extraordinary few who not only escape poverty but rise to the top and become wealthy. The exceptions can lead us to believe that poverty is optional and that anyone can get out. What about those who don't? Are they perpetually poor because of poor choices or lack of initiative?

In these verses we see that poverty is perpetuated by injustice despite hard work and, in the last proverb, we see a hard truth: God is the maker of the poor. I believe that not only means God is their Creator, but also God has created a special group of people – the poor – to serve many purposes in His plan.

Despite the compelling pitches of many social services organizations, the hard fact is that you and I can't solve the problem of poverty and neither can poor people themselves. What we can do is be kind to poor people. We can give to organizations that provide relief, we can give to people who, despite significant personal efforts, have dire financial needs. We may have someone like that in our own family – it might be one of our grandparents. There are many elderly who are living only from their Social Security benefits and are unable to afford even necessities.

We can also try to give whenever we're asked. It's utterly humiliating to ask for charity, and to be turned down burns in the soul. If we cannot give what is being asked of us because we know it's not wise or will jeopardize our own welfare, can't we give something? Let's consider our many resources and try to give something. Our kindness honors God.

Hold this thought: I will treat everyone with dignity, regardless of their social position.

I Tithed out of Desperation

One woman gives freely, yet gains even more; another withholds unduly, but comes to poverty.
A generous woman will prosper; she who refreshes others will her-self be refreshed.
People curse the woman who hoards grain, but blessings crown her who is willing to sell.

Proverbs 11:24-26

A stingy woman is eager to get rich and is unaware that poverty awaits her.

197

Proverbs 28:22

Why is it that one woman who gives freely gains even more and another who withholds unduly comes to poverty? Are those women fulfilling their destinies? Was one born to be rich and generous and the other poor and miserly? Look, the next verse answers the question – a generous woman – any generous woman – will prosper. So all I have to do is be generous?

That's easy enough for someone with money, but what about when we don't have enough to pay our bills? It's not "withhold-ing unduly" when we need for ourselves, is it? There are times in life when income is so tight that it hardly seems possible to give.

Yet when we need money the most is when we must learn to give. Giving in our time of need is the only way we'll ever get out from under a constant state of never having enough.

The Bible promises great blessings if we'll give to church and charity a tenth of our gross income – otherwise known as tith-ing. God said it and I believe it: if we tithe, we will always have enough. There may be financial road bumps, but even if we have a great financial loss, God will take care of His children

---

On the other hand, what can a Christian who doesn't tithe expect? She may never be able to make ends meet, let alone get the slightest bit ahead. Just when she thinks she will finally have enough money to pay her bills, something else unexpected comes up. Try as she might, she will not get it right. That's because she's not following the first rule of good financial management – generosity.

Hey, I know it's hard. It scares me sometimes to see that I'm giving as much away to church and charity as my house payment costs. Sometimes I think how my family could use that money, but that's a fleeting temptation of the devil because I quickly realize that if God hadn't blessed me the way He has, 10 percent of my income would not be such an impressive figure!

At the time I made a decision to tithe, one-tenth of my monthly income was exactly $45. We're talking serious poverty! When I subtracted out a student loan payment and car insurance from my gross income as well, I had very little money left to live on. Outside of my Peace Corps experience, it's the least amount of money I've had to live on as an adult – and I had a child to support too. Our basic needs were met because I was taking care of my grandparents and "compensation" for that "job" was room and board. That didn't put gas in my car or buy my kid clothes or a birthday present though. I really needed more money and I didn't know how to go about bringing it in – I could not get a regular job because I had two grandparents and a four-year-old to care for at home. I made the decision to tithe because of the difficult financial fix I was in. I couldn't think of anything else to do; I might

> At the time I made a decision to tithe, one-tenth of my monthly income was exactly $45. We're talking serious poverty!

as well take God up on His offer!

The pastor of the church I was attending was doing a series of sermons on tithing and if you've ever heard one of those, you know what that sounds like. The person who tithes is sitting in the pews nodding her head saying, "Amen, Brother!" and the person who doesn't tithe is getting hot under the collar – and maybe thinking: "Greedy buggers. This church doesn't need any more money!"

I was sitting in the pews that day in a neutral frame of mind, if not a bit worried because of my very low income. The pastor pointed out that God invites us to try Him in this one aspect of life – "Try me in this" (Malachi 3:10), God says; tithe and God will start pouring out blessings. I had already figured out by this time that I wasn't going to win the lottery, so I thought this was my best bet for a big turnaround.

Not a month after I paid my first tithe, I found a perfect part-time job writing features for a small, weekly newspaper in a neighboring county. I could take my daughter and only needed to be gone a few hours on one day a week to do interviews – then I wrote at home. And in a few months more, I picked up another writing job for a monthly paper in my own town. Then, money started coming in from many places, most notably from my aunt and uncles who gave me substantial gifts of appreciation for my care of their parents. Fifteen months later, I had paid off the rest of my student loan (twice as quickly as I was scheduled to do) and, if you can believe this, I had quit my weekly newspaper job because I didn't need the money!

Now less than 10 years later, I own a beautiful home, have money saved and I make more money working from the comfort of my home than I have ever made anywhere. You can bet I'm a believer in tithing. And not just that, but going beyond tithing, too.

A tithe is a base of giving. For a base salary and a base lifestyle, give the base tithe. But if we want bigger blessings, we must give beyond the base – we need to give of our time, talents, other resources and, yep, even more money. These other gifts are called offerings. God loved them in the Old Testament and though we don't hear as much about them in the New Testament, we do see continuous urgings to give, give, give. Jesus said, "If you want to be perfect, go, sell your possessions and give to the poor" (Matthew 19:21).

Perfection! Now there's a goal.

200 *Hold this thought: God gives money back with interest.*

chapter eight

The E³ (Ethereal•Ephemeral•Eternal) Wisdom of the Proverbs

Looking for Treasure in Verbal Spewage

"Diamonds are a Girl's Best Friend"

Bite Your Tongue!

Good King Sol vs. Jeff Foxworthy

You've Been Punked!

Looking for Treasure in Verbal Spewage

Whoever loves discipline loves knowledge, but she who hates correction is stupid.

Proverbs 12:1

The way of a fool seems right to her, but a wise woman listens to advice.

Proverbs 12:15

Pride only breeds quarrels, but wisdom is found in those who take advice.

Proverbs 13:10

Whoever gives heed to instruction prospers, and blessed is she who trusts in the Lord.

Proverbs 16:20

One of the most useful skills to our success in life will be the ability to take advice. If we can master this, it will set us apart and propel us forward in career, society and our personal relationships. Advice is all around us, but so few people take advantage of it. There are self-help and how-to books a plenty. But are they read? During my engagement, I bought *The Idiot's Guide to the Perfect Marriage.* I've never read it, but probably need to!

If we want to distinguish ourselves in this life, determine to learn from others.

When we find ourselves needing advice, most of us will readily turn to a book. What are books but other people's knowledge and advice? We are willing to learn from books, but when it comes to learning from people directly – without the degree of separation that a book inserts, we are so resistant. We don't like taking advice from the people in our lives. Pride may overtake us when people are involved in the teaching. It's difficult to acknowledge that someone else can help us become a better person. But isn't that always the way self-improvement happens? It only makes sense to open ourselves up to as much knowledge and instruction as we can to become the best people we can be.

I believe most people are resistant to correction and advice because it usually comes as a negative response to something we have done. Good advice sometimes sounds exactly like criticism – or worse – like scolding.

One afternoon during my junior year of high school, I was working on a journalism project with other students in a small class of about 10. We were having some fun with it and being somewhat boisterous, all of us except the teacher who was working in her office. All of the sudden, from her office she shouted, "Donna, lower your voice! Your voice has a very annoying quality to it!"

Out of a low roar of intermingled voices, she found mine to criticize – and not the least bit discreetly. Of course, I was humiliated. When I got over the embarrassment (which took a while), I found some good advice in what she said. I started to listen to myself and found that when I wanted to be heard over the rest, I did put a shrill edge on my voice that cut through air like a chain saw!

I began to work on controlling the quality of my voice and I believe I have a much more pleasant "crowd" voice now – thanks to an insult hurled at me in a moment of frustration! That was an early experience that helped me develop an ability to listen to (not just hear) people who are criticizing me or giving me advice.

When someone starts in on me, I try to brace myself and think, "OK, I'm just going to listen to this and see if there is something valuable in it." I hear the words as if they are directed to someone else, not me. I have to stop feeling and just take notes. Later, I let myself feel all the emotions that criticism stirs. If I don't control those emotions when I'm listening, I miss important information. The hurtful words can keep me from seeing the spirit in which they are being delivered or hearing the more subtle statements that sound almost like afterthoughts but are really the crux of the matter.

Let's bring our analytical thought into action as we listen to advice and especially criticism. Think of it as a treasure hunt. In all those words, there might be something very valuable. Listen carefully, sort through it and it could have a big payoff!

Hold this thought: Listen for the gems.

"Diamonds are a Girl's Best Friend"

My daughter, if you accept my words and store up my commands within you, turning your ear to wisdom and applying your heart to understanding, and if you call out for insight and cry aloud for understanding, and if you look for it as for silver and search for it as for hidden treasure, then you will understand the fear of the Lord and find the knowledge of God. For the Lord gives wisdom, and from his mouth come knowledge and understanding.

Proverbs 2:1-6

205

When you were young, you used to love a treasure hunt. How do I know? All children love treasure hunts. There is something in us that innately loves the prospect of coming upon something valuable in an unexpected place. It's the same force that makes some people pore over flea markets looking for an inadvertently discarded collector's item and other people pore over the finance page of the newspaper looking for that one stock that might take off and make them a millionaire. We're hardwired to search for valuable things. If you can channel that natural treasure-hunting force within you to seek spiritual jewels, what you find will be of immeasurable value to your life.

In my youth, I studied God's word with the same enthusiasm with which I take vitamins. I knew it was good for me and so I disciplined myself to do it. After some time, my discipline waned and my sense of duty weakened and I stopped studying the Bible regularly – and then not long after that, I stopped studying it all together.

After many years without faithfully reading the Bible, I decided one day to open up the book to any page just to see if there was something there for me. To my great surprise, there was. The first verse I set my eyes on had special meaning for me. I shut the book.

That verse was a mindful and I chewed on it mentally for several days. Then I began to wonder what would happen if I randomly opened the book again. Could I possibly find another jewel? So I tried it again, and it worked. Again, my eyes landed right on another special message from God to me.

I think God was putting these jewels just where I would look to encourage me to turn back to the Bible. God knew I needed to be convinced of God's ability to speak to me through the Bible. After a few more such experiences, I decided to start from the beginning of the Bible and read it with the goal of getting to know my Heavenly Father. From the very first day, God revealed new secrets to me that I had not seen the first time I read the Bible – when my goal was simply to read the whole Bible.

Once I accepted that God does speak through words, I began to search for special written messages. Many people have been inspired of God to write their life experiences, devotional guides and even novels that God can use to teach us. I now spend a good deal of time in a search for the treasure of God's special messages for me and I have not been disappointed with my finds.

I think God rewards people who seek Him out of a sense of discipline and duty, but I think God delights in people who seek Him with a sense of adventure and excitement. Sometimes, if I have a special question that is puzzling me, like wondering how I should decide on some important issue, I ask God to speak clearly to me with an answer. I cannot expect God to answer me through a Stephen King novel or an episode of "Desperate Housewives." I have to search, like a real treasure hunt, in places I think God might place a jewel. I search the Word; I listen to my favorite people of God such as my local pastor; I ask my mother or some other Godly person whose opinion I respect; I read books that might hold the answer. When God gives me a specific answer I've been looking for, I usually document it as the miracle that it is on my blog www.iBelieveinMiracles.info. Check it out and please add miracles you've experienced to the blog.

Unlike the mostly futile search through the flea market and stock market, when we search diligently for wisdom and understanding, the promise God gives in this proverb is that we will find what we are searching for – and more. With our find, we learn to respect God more, God gives us knowledge – we actually get smarter – and God helps us to understand things we did not understand before. We get all that plus the answer we were looking for. What a find!

207

What are you searching for? What are you trying to find on eBay or in the mall or even on a nature trail? How about adding wisdom and understanding to the things you routinely keep an eye out for? Here are a few suggestions:

- Sign up for a list serv or bookmark a favorite Web site to daily search for spiritual jewels.
- Keep a devotional book in the bathroom to search through in your "down" time.
- Fill your house with materials and your daily routine with opportunities to look for and find spiritual jewels.

Hold this thought: I'm on a treasure hunt for wisdom.

Bite Your Tongue!

The wise in heart accept commands, but a chattering fool comes to ruin.

Proverbs 10:8

Wise women store up knowledge, but the mouth of a fool invites ruin.

Proverbs 10:14

When words are many, sin is not absent, but she who holds her tongue is wise.

Proverbs 10:19

A person who lacks judgment derides her neighbor, but a woman of understanding holds her tongue.

Proverbs 11:12

A prudent woman keeps her knowledge to herself, but the heart of fools blurts out folly.

Proverbs 12:23

She who guards her lips guards her life, but she who speaks rashly will come to ruin.

Proverbs 13:3

Even a fool is thought wise if she keeps silent, and discerning if she holds her tongue.

Proverbs 17:28

One day when I was a teenager, I went with my dad to his friend's house. I didn't know the man so I sat quietly as they visited. I was probably daydreaming about one of my get-rich-quick schemes even though I was looking at my father's friend as he spoke. All of the sudden he turned to me and said, "You must be a very wise girl. You're just sitting there taking this all in." Though I'm sure that compliment was not merited, his comment stuck with me.

Some months later, I was at home with my dad and he was lecturing me about something (bla, bla, bla). This time, I was not sitting quietly and taking it all in. Instead, I was following him around raising every objection I could think of to whatever it was we were arguing about. All of the sudden he turned to me and said, "You would have made a good Olive Oyl." (Remember, Popeye the Sailor's loud-mouthed girlfriend?) That one I deserved and it stuck with me, as well.

If we want people to think we are wise, what we need to do is shut up and listen. We can fool a lot of people that way, right? Wrong! If we shut up and listen, we won't just make others think we're wise – we will actually be wise!

During trying circumstances and trouble when we do not know what to do, we wish for wisdom – instant wisdom. "God, help me to know what to do!" we might be crying on the inside. Wouldn't it be great if we could instantly tap into the wisdom of God in any situation? Guess what. We can! The power is in our silence.

When we don't know what to say or do, just be quiet. When we're distraught, when we're angry, when we feel betrayed, when we've been cheated, when we're stressed out, when we feel awkward, when someone is yelling at us – whatever the situation – the wisest thing we can do is be quiet. Repeat our plea to God in our mind, "God, help me to know what to do!" and then listen with our mind and heart.

We have all reflected on a quarrel we had and thought to ourselves, "I wish I had said …" The brilliant retorts always seem to come to us just after the crisis is over. Why is that? Could that mental block in the heat of the argument be God's hand over our mouth? Is God protecting us from foolish impulses? What would have been the net result of blurting out a dead-on, hurtful comeback before we walked out the door? Would the person we had the conflict with think more highly of us? Would that cutting remark have improved our situation or brought us closer to a resolution with that person?

Thank God for the times we can't think of that quick comeback. And even when we can, let's pray we have the instant wisdom to keep our mouths shut.

Hold this thought: Better to keep quiet.

Good King Sol vs. Jeff Foxworthy

Pay attention and listen to the sayings of the wise; apply your heart to what I teach, for it is pleasing when you keep them in your heart and have all of them ready on your lips. So that your trust may be in the Lord, I teach you today, even you. Have I not written thirty sayings for you, sayings of counsel and knowledge, teaching you true and reliable words, so that you can give sound answers…?

Proverbs 22:17-21

211

Our minds, brilliant as they are, aren't steel traps. They are more like colanders. They catch the big chunks and let a lot of other stuff wash through. If we want to grow in wisdom, we have to compensate for the colander effect and keep adding fresh material all the time.

I find it funny and sad that in the verse above, the sage says, "Haven't I given you thirty sayings?" Thirty sayings sure doesn't seem like much. I'm supposed to navigate life with 30 sayings? That's almost laughable. The sad part is that even with such a brief instruction book, just 30 sayings, I haven't memorized it! You would think that if my happiness and success depended on 30 tidbits of wisdom, I could memorize those.

Yet, I carry the preamble to the U.S. Constitution ready on my lips, the first sentence of the Gettysburg Address, JFK's famous "Ask not" quote and yes, a whole lot of completely meaningless lines from movies.

For every "Show me the money" you have memorized, do you have a Biblical match – such as "Seek first the kingdom of God and its righteousness and all these things will be added to you"? Listen to yourself for a few days and take note of what you're regurgitating verbatim. Do you have instructions from God's manual that will help you make wise decisions when you're at life's crossroads? Or are you full of blue-collar comedy? Compare how many versions of "You might be a redneck if..." you can recite to how many proverbs you can quote.

I don't know about you, but in my time of distress, Jeff Fox-worthy's humor is nothing more than a distraction. I can't recall a time his or anyone else's brand of humor helped me make a wise decision. Decision-making is just the sort of thing for which I need some good advice in reserve! If all I have is stale jokes and movie quotes swimming around in my noggin, I'm up the creek!

Don't underestimate the difficulty of making good decisions in life. To me, deciding wisely is the most difficult thing in a Christian walk. It's harder than resisting temptation, because when we're tempted, we usually know quite well what the right thing to do is. Then, it's just a matter of making the choice to act in a way we already know is right. The instructions on that one are pretty clear too, "Resist temptation and it will flee from you." However in decision-making, that strategy doesn't work. The decision won't go away if we resist making it. And Satan's devices to trip us up are a lot more subtle. Sometimes all our options seem wrong and we have to choose the lesser of two evils. Sometimes the wrong decision (the one Satan wants us to choose) is disguised as good, and the truly good choice may appear in the eyes of the

I'm supposed to navigate life with 30 sayings? That's almost laughable. The sad part is that even with such a brief instruction book, just 30 sayings, I haven't memorized it! You would think that if my happiness and success depended on 30 tidbits of wisdom, I could memorize those.

world to be cruel, inflexible and negative.

In these times of total confusion, we need directions, not distractions! And if we have instructions stored away in our memory, God will bring them to mind to help us make the right choice.

Hold this thought: I will commit some scripture to memory.

213

You've Been Punked!

Do you see a woman wise in her own eyes? There is more hope for a fool than for her.
The sluggard is wiser in her own eyes than seven women who answer wisely.

Proverbs 26:12, 16

Here's a great irony – just when we think we're wise, we're not! Proverbs urges us continually to get wisdom and understanding then it slaps this on us. "You think you got it? You've been punked!"

And what about me? How is an unwise person supposed to write a commentary on the Proverbs? And yet, considering our verse, I would hardly want to think myself wise.

In English, we say, "be wise" and "become wise," but we really should talk more in terms of having wisdom. If we "are wise," it is only in the same sense that we "are well-rested" or "are full." Wisdom for our soul is like sleep, food and water for our bodies – it requires continual replenishing. If we are wise, it's only for the moment in which God grants us a good measure of His wisdom. If we want to remain wise, we have to stay tapped into the only source of wisdom – our Heavenly Father.

I think of wisdom like holding water in my hands. I get my hands full of it, and try as I might, it has a way of slipping through my hands. If I want to continually have wisdom, I pretty much have to hold my hands under the tap.

That concept takes a little getting used to. I don't like it, in fact. It reminds me of making my bed. I do it reluctantly thinking, "I'm just going to mess it up later and have to do this same thing again tomorrow. And why bother? I'm leaving the house and not even going to see it all day."

Wouldn't it be great if wisdom were like knowledge? When I learn something new about computers, for example, I have that information in my brain for a good long while. Even if the technology becomes obsolete and I have no use for the information, I can still remember the old way of doing things – like threading an old dot matrix printer (before your day). I add knowledge of the new technology on the foundation of the knowledge of the old. Knowledge forms something like a mental stalactite, but wisdom is running water that we are powerless to dam.

So we have to get wisdom everyday. We need to fill our day with opportunities to tap into the only source of wisdom. We start the day with the Word of God, and throughout the day, add a little God-inspired writing, music, art, preaching and don't forget to still your mind for a chance to receive direct relays from our Heavenly Father Himself. Staying in this perpetual plugged-in state is about as wise as a person can be.

Yet something interesting happens when we're plugged in. When we stand before the Creator of the universe, we are humbled. We get a glimpse of how awesome God is and we realize how insignificant we are. These facts don't make us feel wise, they make us feel like we've won the lottery to be called a daughter of God. On a cosmic scale, we're not even as significant as a single cell here on Earth, yet the Creator of the universe calls us "daughter." Wow.

Our only significance is in our relationship with the

> I think of wisdom like holding water in my hands. I get my hands full of it, and try as I might, it has a way of slipping through my hands. If I want to continually have wisdom, I pretty much have to hold my hands under the tap.

215

Creator. When we acknowledge this, when those foolish illusions of grandeur are gone, then God can use us.

Hold this thought: Only a fool thinks she is wise.

216

chapter nine

Long-Term Forecast: Sunny Skies

The Consequential Krispy Kreme

Brazen Hussy or Wisdom Herself?

Puppy Power, Old Hound Dog Perspective   217

Who's Really to Blame?

Make it Stick

Hang Tough!

Keep an Eye out for Snakes
and Other Distortions of Reality

Time to Buy a New Car, God Willing

The Consequential Krispy Kreme

Wisdom calls aloud in the street, she raises her voice in the public squares; at the head of the noisy streets she cries out, in the gateways of the city she makes her speech; "How long will you simple ones love your simple ways? How long will mockers delight in mockery and fools hate knowledge? If you had responded to my rebuke, I would have poured out my heart to you and made my thoughts known to you. But since you rejected me when I called and no one gave heed when I stretched out my hand, since you ignored all my advice and would not accept my rebuke, I in turn will laugh at your disaster; I will mock when calamity overtakes you – when calamity overtakes you like a storm, when disaster sweeps over you like a whirlwind, when distress and trouble overwhelm you. Then they will call to me but I will not answer; they will look for me but will not find me. Since they hated knowledge and did not choose to fear the Lord, since they would not accept my advice and spurned my rebuke, they will eat the fruit of their schemes. For the waywardness of the simple will kill them, and the complacency of fools will destroy them; but whoever listens to me will live in safety and be at ease, without fear of harm."

Proverbs 1:20-33

Solomon, the same man who in the book of Ecclesiastes said he never met a wise woman, compensates for that egregious claim by portraying wisdom in the form of a woman, and in the passage above, we get a glimpse of the way "she" operates.

Personally, I see Ms. Wisdom as an exotic, wispy, large, transparent creature, beautiful beyond words, floating through the streets, houses, buildings, farms and forests, whispering counsel to each person as a desire rises up in them. I hear her sweet voice quite often and if you pay attention, you will recognize her as well. She is there calling to us all in the very moment we need to hear her.

For instance, I am driving down the road and I spot a Krispy Kreme shop just ahead. A desire stirs within me. "You'll be having lunch in an hour," Wisdom whispers. I ignore her. Before I know it, I'm in the drive-thru, blocked from behind by two other cars. The only way out is through the check-out.

A raspy voice comes over the speaker. "Welcome to Krispy Kreme. We're offering two dozen donuts for a special price of $6. Would you like to take some to your co-workers or family?" I'm waving Wisdom off as she insists I don't need that many donuts. I'm feeling generous. I want my family and co-workers to feel the thrill of the glazed donut too. "Yes," I say, "I'll take that."

Swoosh! Off flies Wisdom, disgusted with me. She has left me to my own devices. I eat about four of those 24 donuts. I only really wanted one donut and I didn't even need that. Some co-workers have one or two. About half of the donuts turn hard and crusty.

The next morning, I step on the scale and am appalled. I haven't lost any weight. But I worked out yesterday. How can this be? I'm so depressed. Out of the corner of my eye, I see Wisdom with her eyes rolled way back in her head, jaw clenched, shaking her head from side to side. "Moron!" she must be thinking.

It is only natural for this animal body to want what will make us feel good at the moment – sleep, a donut, vegging out in front of the television, pizza at midnight. Our natural emotions cause us to want to feel important, intimate with another person, secure and sometimes we just don't want to feel anything – we just want to have fun and get our minds off our boredom or problems. None of our physical or emotional desires are bad – God designed us to want all of those things. However, each can be satisfied in a wise way or a foolish way.

Glutting on donuts is not a life or death situation, but it is a real-life situation. Whether you give in to donuts, pizza, sleep, procrastination, sex or staying in a bad relationship because it offers some security, making wrong choices always has negative consequences. Solomon writes often of this throughout Proverbs. It is a very simple truth that most of us need a lot of convincing to accept.

Hold this thought: Bad decisions bring negative consequences.

220

Brazen Hussy or Wisdom Herself?

At the window of my house I looked out through the lattice. I saw among the simple, I noticed among the young men, a youth who lacked judgment. He was going down the street near her corner, walking along in the direction of her house at twilight, as the day was fading, as the dark of night set in. Then out came a woman to meet him, dressed like a prostitute and with crafty intent. (She is loud and defiant, her feet never stay at home; now in the street, now in the squares, at every corner she lurks.) She took hold of him and kissed him and with a brazen face she said: "I have fellowship offerings at home: today I fulfilled my vows. So I came out to meet you; I looked for you and have found you! I have covered my bed with colored linens from Egypt. I have perfumed my bed with myrrh, aloes and cinnamon."

221

Proverbs 7:1-17

Does not wisdom call out? Does not understanding raise her voice? On the heights along the way, where the paths meet, she takes her stand; beside the gates leading into the city, at the entrances, she cries aloud; "To you, O men, I call out: I raise my voice to all mankind. You who are simple, gain prudence; you who are foolish, gain understanding. Listen, for I have worthy things to say; I open my lips to speak what is right. My mouth speaks what is true, for my lips detest wickedness. … I, wisdom, dwell with prudence; I possess knowledge and discretion. To fear the Lord is to hate evil; I hate pride and arrogance, evil behavior and perverse speech. Counsel and sound judgment are mine. I have understanding and power. … I love those who love me, and those who seek me find me. … I walk in the way of righteousness along the paths of justice…"

Proverbs 8:1-7, 12-14, 17, 20

Whereas most people read these passages and see the general advice to steer clear of the seductresses in favor of wisdom, for young women, these passages hold something more – a study in opposites. Let's do a little compare and contrast between Brazen Hussy (sounds like a name out of a James Bond movie!) and Wisdom Herself.

Characteristic	Brazen Hussy	Wisdom Herself
Waking hours	Nocturnal – comes out at twilight	Diurnal – works during high traffic hours
Lives with…	Her husband	A roommate – Prudence.
Appearance	Dresses in revealing clothing	Discreet
Demeanor	Talks and laughs loudly; has a rebellious attitude	Talks loud; humble; well-behaved
Toward men acts…	Sexually aggressive	Professionally aggressive
Pastimes	Loitering – lurks at every corner	Walking – prefers the paths of justice
Spends her resources to get…	Silk sheets and love potions	Knowledge, counsel, sound judgment, understanding, power
Values	Mocks traditions, unfaithful to spouse	Family-oriented ("love those who love me")

We have here two young women who can both be described as socially assertive, impassioned women, though with very different motivations. Brazen Hussy is focused on scouting men, adding notches to her bedpost and perfecting a lingerie-model persona. Wisdom's crusade is to help people to become prudent and gain understanding.

It's interesting to note that Wisdom is not a timid, submissive woman. She is humble but self-assured. She boldly states her convictions, her likes and dislikes. She is very much in the public eye. She's a learned woman, a powerful woman, she has good judgment and discretion and people seek her out for advice. This doesn't sound very much like the image of the bread-baking, closed-mouth, good Christian woman that I grew up with. But this definitely sounds like someone I would like to be.

223

Sadly, today's typical young American woman better fits the profile of Brazen Hussy – always hanging out in the mall looking for a new thong, staying out late and sleeping late. "Revealing" is a quality she looks for in clothes, and her body language and speech are so exaggerated that she is a parody of herself. The only passion she knows is lust – a tragic waste of potential.

How about you? If you had to place yourself in one of the two columns above, which would it be? Are you about your business during the day or are you sleeping off the night before? Is your attitude generally rebellious and mocking or is it respectful and compassionate? What do you spend your resources (time, energy, money) acquiring – things that will make you more attractive and cool or things that will build your character? Do you have positive purpose?

One of God's gifts to us during our late teen years, that last hallmark of development, is a well of passion and energy, along with the feeling that we can do anything. I believe God gives this to us to help us be positive agents of change in the world. There are always old ways of doing things that need to be challenged and changed – outdated thinking and technology. Youth keep the wheel of humanity churning with their innovative thinking and desire to make a mark on the world. That's in the best of scenarios.

More often, youth do not know what to do with all that God-given passion. Maybe we lack positive role models in our immediate environment, or maybe our lives have been so sheltered, and so much has been provided for us that we are satisfied and cannot even identify something close to us that needs positive change. Some find an outlet in art, music, dance, technology and self-expression on the Internet and other venues. For those less fortunate that have not even discovered a creative outlet, there is the default passion of humanity – lust.

This most base passion will fill the vacuum in the life of a youth if no other outlet for youthful passion and energy takes root. Let me put it another way – sex as a hobby is for people who haven't found anything better to do.

Everyone has sexual desire – even those who are using our youthful passion for just causes. The difference is that for a person with a passion for lust, sex is the focal point of life. For the rest of us, sexual desire has an appropriate, balanced place in our lives – it enhances and enriches our lives but we don't schedule our day around it.

Let's not waste our gift of energy on the common denominator between us and the animals! Find a higher purpose, a positive outlet for our God-given youthful energy and optimism. Pick up a *Newsweek* to learn about a dozen injustices we can throw ourselves in to. Pick up a phone book and find the social service organizations in our towns. Visit the rape crisis center, the homeless shelter, a children's home, a cancer ward. Let's pour ourselves into something that will make the world a better place. Let's use our passion wisely.

Hold this thought: I want to use my passion to make a positive impact.

Puppy Power, Old Hound Dog Perspective

It is not good to have zeal without knowledge or be hasty and miss the way.

Proverbs 19:2

Consider a puppy, maybe a chocolate Labrador about 12 weeks old. Except for when it crashes to nap, that animal is 100 percent positive energy at all times. What enthusiasm! Puppies always seem so happy to just be! And if they've been raised in a loving family, they love everyone. Don't you sometimes wish you could bottle and take a daily dose of a puppy's *je ne sais quoi*? After a good stretch, I would love to just run around being happy from one person to the next – pause to gobble a meal – then run around and play some more. That's zeal.

Our same chocolate Lab pup runs down the driveway to jump up on Grandma when she comes to visit and knocks down toddlers just to say "hello." The pup doesn't know where she should and shouldn't go potty yet, nor the difference between a chew toy and our favorite leather accessory. And it's all the same to her if she digs a nice cool spot in the dirt in a discreet place on the edge of the yard or right in the middle of our neighbor's flower bed.

Puppies are such great fun, and it takes all of about 10 minutes for them to sink roots in our hearts. However, after a couple of days of cleaning dog poop from inconvenient places, we know our puppy must grow in knowledge as it grows in size if the two of us are to have a future together. For starters, our puppy is going to have to learn to discriminate between our shoes and a rawhide chew. This process of imparting knowledge to our puppy takes time, patience and consistency on our part. Each minute we invest in purposefully and lovingly teaching our puppy how to live successfully with us is well spent and will

225

eventually pay off in the form of a loyal, loving companion who won't knock Grandma down when she comes to visit.

I don't recall ever knocking Grandma down, but there have been plenty of times in my life that I was highly enthusiastic and eager to make a mark of a human kind, and rushed in with that puppy zeal only to make a fine mess of things.

My first month on the job as executive director of Hope House of Savannah, I received a notice of a meeting in which the directors of the social services for the city's homeless would have the chance to prioritize the needs and service gaps in our city and then draft a plan to address some of the needs with federal grant money. I had dreamed of being an executive director for a long time, and now here I was and this was my first opportunity to make a real impact. Hope House wanted to grow and address more of the community's needs and this meeting seemed like a good place to start.

On the day of the meeting, the gathered directors made a needs list. One of Hope House's specialties was high on the list – more housing for families (versus single, homeless men and women). Later, when it came to making the plan of how to address the needs, I asserted early on that Hope House would like to help address that top priority need. However, as we further discussed how the federal grant monies would be used, it became clear to me that several people around the table had already had some extensive discussion prior to the meeting. That might have been OK except for one thing: The programs for which they intended to use the federal

> I had believed that fateful meeting to be a lush, green meadow of opportunity. What I didn't know is that it was littered with cow patties, and I stepped full into a big squishy one.

funds did not match the list of needs we had identified earlier. They wanted to fund a lawyer for the local legal aid office with the new grant money. Legal aid was on the list of needs, but somewhere buried in the lower quarter. I thought that was dirty dealing. And though I didn't come right out and accuse the other directors of that at the meeting, I did take a very zealous stand for using the money to address the top priority needs, as we had been directed to do, and I staunchly opposed using it for another legal aid lawyer. In the end, I was outnumbered. Oh well, right? I did what I could but the "good old boy" network prevailed.

Was I wrong? No. However, I had zeal without knowledge and my ignorance cost my agency dearly. What I didn't know was that some of those key people I was zealously opposing would later review Hope House's grant application for city funds. That, in itself is a conflict of interest as some of them also received city funds, but that was also, in itself, reality. In the next city grant cycle, I was shocked to find our funding reduced by $10,000 with no explanation.

I had believed that fateful meeting to be a lush, green meadow of opportunity. What I didn't know is that it was littered with cow patties, and I stepped full into a big squishy one. It took a long time to scrape all the poop off my shoe (figuratively speaking). I had to learn how to collaborate with these other community leaders for whom I now lacked respect. I had to win their confidence *back*, which was much harder than it would have been to win it to begin with. And I had to do double-time to come up with ways to recuperate the funding Hope House lost. I did – with zeal *and* knowledge.

Hold this thought: Before I charge in with zeal, I learn where I can safely step!

Who's Really to Blame?

A woman's own folly ruins her life, yet her heart rages against the Lord.

Proverbs 19:3

Have you ever had a premonition that something was going to go wrong? Maybe you only realized it after everything was said and done. In retrospect you reflect, "I knew there was something not right about that. I had a strange feeling about that." Learn to pay attention to that sixth sense we so often ignore and our culture denies even exists. Trust that voice.

Ironically, many young women will cue into my advice about the sixth sense and put great effort into becoming attuned to their intuition while turning a blind eye and deaf ear to good advice being broadcast around them. Don't make that mistake. Intuition is another one of the senses and should be used in conjunction with the others, just as we use our sight in conjunction with our hearing to be able, for instance, to locate the telephone when it rings. Likewise, we must use our intuition *with* our reliable eyesight, hearing and conscious thought processes – don't spurn the obvious in deference to intuition.

Use the input from all our senses, to do what? Make good decisions. That is the key here, it's what this verse, and in fact, this book is all about! After our basic profession of faith, making good decisions is the most important thing for this very moment, every day and our entire lives. For instance, if we're reading this book while we should be walking out the door to get to work on time, we're in need of a good decision. Put the book down! Go to work! (If not, read on.)

There's a great story in the book of Joshua that so well illustrates how our choices bring ruin on us and how, if we are truly sorry for our foolishness and seek God, God is faithful to use that same folly to our advantage.

The Israelites had just pummeled Jericho, and basking in the glory of this incredible and divine victory, they set their sites on a little place called Ai. It was such a spit of a town that Israeli scouts recommended sending only 3,000 troops to finish it off. So Joshua commanded it and off they went. He felt very confident as God had promised him over and over that He would be with him every step of the way, giving him victory.

What Joshua didn't know was that the people of Israel (as a whole) were not right before God. They had a hidden sin. Some idiot from the tribe of Judah just couldn't restrain himself and tried to keep some of the plunder from Jericho – something God had strictly forbidden. This guy had buried in his tent a fine cloak, 200 shekels of silver and a bar of gold. Jericho was Israel's first victory in Canaan. If God were to allow this disobedience to go unnoticed, what would stop others from doing the same thing? God had to nip this disobedience in the bud!

God got Joshua's attention with a humiliating defeat at Ai. That scrawny town chased away the 3,000 Israeli troops – sent them packing with tails between their legs – and killed 36 of them. When Joshua got this news, he threw a fit, literally. He flailed on the ground tearing his clothes and throwing dirt in his hair and then began to rage against God: "Why did you ever bring this people across the Jordan to deliver us into the hands of the Amorites to destroy us? If only we had been content to stay on the other side of the Jordan!" And on and on (read the full story, Joshua 7 and 8).

I love how God replied to Joshua: "Stand up. What are you doing on your face?" (I can almost hear God saying that to me sometimes.) Then God tells Joshua, "Israel has sinned; they violated my covenant which I commanded them to keep." God instructed Joshua how to make things right. The idiot from Judah was found out and his fate was to be an example of why the rest of Israel did not want to disobey God.

Once Israel went through the painful process of setting things right, God renewed the commitment to Joshua and the people and told them to attack Ai again. And here's the beautiful part. God used that previous defeat, the result of Israel's disobedience, to their advantage now that they were right with God again.

Joshua split the army – some to go to the rear of the city and hide, and another large group to attack from the front as they had before. The plan was that when the people of Ai came out to fight, the Israelis would act as if they were going to retreat like they did the first time. They were counting on the people of Ai to chase them like they did before. When they had lured the people away from the town, they would send in the rear guard and burn the city. It worked like a charm. As soon as the rear guard set the city on fire, the troops in front stopped retreating and turned to fight. The people of Ai were trapped and their fate was sealed.

The Ai-ites would have never fallen for such a scheme if they hadn't chased the Israelis down previously. Only because of that previous "ruin" experience did this strategy of luring them out of the city now produce a total victory.

This is great news for you and me. The message is that even after we've screwed up (maybe even unknowingly) and things are in ruins and even after we rage against God for something that is really our own fault, if we will just turn, in humility, and seek God and follow His commands for getting our life back on track, God is gracious and faithful to work even our previous humiliating defeat into an eventual victory for us.

Hold this thought: When I'm in trouble, I'll examine my recent choices rather than rage against the Creator.

230

Make it Stick

It is a trap for a woman to dedicate something rashly and only later to consider her vows.

Proverbs 20:25

When my daughter turned two, I wanted to get her a puppy for her birthday. I had a fenced back yard and the financial resources to be able to feed and care for a dog. I had this thought out and was ready to make the commitment. When an animal-lover friend of mine learned of my plans, she told me about two adorable puppies at her vet's office that needed a home. Two? Yes, one dog gets so lonely by itself, especially if you're gone from home a lot. The animals were free and even spayed, neutered and had their shots. I was sold.

231

The dogs were loving and energetic and we spent our first weekend together getting used to each other. All was well. Then Monday came. When I got home on Monday evening, the dogs were nowhere to be found; they had escaped the back yard. After much calling and canvassing the neighborhood, we found them. That initiated a series of breakouts and subsequent repair jobs to mend the fence or fill the hole where the dogs had escaped. After about three weeks of that almost every weekday, I finally had to admit I could not contain these animals and that was problematic. Besides that, their energy level seemed only to increase the longer we had them. They were in constant motion and forever jumping up on my two-year old and knocking her down. It wasn't working.

I had to abandon my commitment and take the dogs back to the vet. I left the vet's office in tears, partially from the pain of parting with the dogs to which we had become attached and partially out of a feeling of failure. I was 32 years old and couldn't handle two puppies!

Making a commitment, even of the seemingly easy kind like getting a dog, is serious and risky business, and almost everyone screws it up in the course of growing up. A person who honors her commitments is not born, she's formed – through character development, knowledge of self and a little trial and error. It's normal to make commitments we later regret. As we mature, we learn about our staying power and how better to gauge the likelihood we'll be able to honor a commitment.

The key is to not make any major life commitments until we have become a person who can honor a commitment. If our parents have been working to develop this aspect of our character since we were young, we may already be that kind of person. But if one or both or our parents have problems keeping their word, we may have some additional obstacles to overcome in becoming a person who honors commitments; we have to learn behaviors and attitudes that were not modeled for us as a child.

232

Four ways we can develop in ourselves the ability to commit are: Ask God to make us a reliable person who can honor commitments; find a good role model and imitate this person's wise behavior; read up on this godly quality from reputable sources and apply what we learn to our lives; and finally, learn from our mistakes.

When we can't keep a commitment, we need to try to figure out what *we did wrong*. I emphasize that because often when we fail to meet a commitment or keep a promise (same thing) we want to blame other people and external factors.

"I could have paid my rent on time if only my car hadn't broken down." The

> As time passes and the humiliation of the failure begins to fade, we must analyze the circumstances realistically and own up to our part in the failure.

real problem here is that I didn't have money set aside for emergencies.

"My fiancé was supposed to help me pay that bill. If we hadn't broken up, I would have been able to pay it." The real problem here is that I took on a financial obligation I could not afford.

"It's just not realistic for a woman to remain a virgin until marriage." The real problem here is that I moved away from God and caved in to temptation.

At moments of failure, we feel bad enough about ourselves, so we look to external factors as a means of self-preservation. Resorting to this self-deception when we first fail may keep us from becoming acutely depressed, particularly if we have low self-esteem. As time passes and the humiliation of the failure begins to fade, we must analyze the circumstances realistically and own up to our part in the failure. We shouldn't loathe ourselves because of what happened – after all we're in good company. I repeat: Everyone has flaked out on a commitment! Instead, let's turn our energies to learning about ourselves and what we can do in the future to become a person who fulfills her commitments.

233

A lot of people out there are walking away from major commitments and not seeming the least bit bothered by it. Broken promises are so common that they are institutionalized. Half of the marriages in the United States end in a broken commitment and the federal court dockets are full of bankruptcies. Although I firmly believe these failures are personally humiliating and devastating to the individuals going through them, they are so common that there is hardly any social shame in them anymore.

So if we're not going to be outcasts, why does it matter if we keep our promises? People might not think any worse of us, but there are other natural consequences that keep following us for years. Defaulting on a credit card or a loan, for instance, is a strike on our credit report for seven years after we've finally paid off what we owe. That seven year curse of bad credit can keep us from getting an apartment, good rates on car insurance, a house, other credit accounts and the list goes on. Whether a financial obligation or a moral one, broken promises leave long and complicated chains of consequences. They are never worth the hassle, hard work or heartache they cause because we did not keep our word in the first place. Look at what the scripture says: "It is a trap." It looks like it's easy enough to walk away from a commitment but, in fact, it's a real struggle to get free of a broken promise.

234

If you need more reason than that (pardon me for sounding like your mother here), keeping promises are important because God says so – that's why! Good King Sol says in another of his books, "When you make a vow to God, do not delay in fulfilling it. He has no pleasure in fools; fulfill your vow. It is better not to vow than to make a vow and not fulfill it. …do not protest… 'My vow was a mistake'" (Ecclesiastes 5:4-6). And this is just one of the many places in the Bible that God instructs us to keep our promises. In fact, a central theme throughout the entire Bible, Old and New Testaments alike, is the covenant (agreement or contract) between God and His children. No doubt, God cares about commitment. When we are fulfilling our part of the divine contract, we walk in harmony with God and enjoy all the benefits of a loving relationship with our Heavenly Father. It works the same way in the material world – we are in harmony with our fellow man when we keep our word.

Become and remain a person who commits herself only after much thought and then honors the commitments she makes. It's an essential godly quality for an abundant life.

Hold this thought: I don't make rash decisions, and when I do decide, I make it stick.

Hang Tough!

If you falter in times of trouble, how small is your strength!
Proverbs 24:10

Peace Corps service is two years, which doesn't sound like very long, but when you've only lived 22 years, two years is a long time – it's about eight percent of your life. Peace Corps recruiters try their best to select volunteers whom they believe can stick out a two-year commitment. I recall the person who interviewed me asked if I had a boyfriend. When I said "no," he cautioned me against getting into any relationships between then and my scheduled departure. Volunteers who leave a sweetheart behind are much less likely to make it through two years, he said.

There were 75 people at my Peace Corps pre-departure orientation and when the two years of Peace Corps service was over, there were fewer than 35 of us left. Over half the group had given up somewhere along the way. Almost all who went home early did so within the first year. After our first-year anniversary, there may have been one or two who left, but for the most part, if they could stick it out the first year, they could make it two years. I don't believe there's any mathematical formula for success in that. It's just that one year is sufficient time to experience some adversity, and in the face of that experience, some faltered, others pressed on.

To be fair, there were a couple of volunteers who cannot be blamed for quitting early, like the young woman who on the night of our swearing in ceremony was abducted, blinded, raped and left for dead on the top of a mountain. She left to save her life. Probably every volunteer was the victim of some crime – mostly petty theft – but her tragedy was by far the most heinous thing to happen to any of us and any Peace Corps volunteer in Ecuador for a long time before and after.

I'm glad to say that I made it through two years without folding, but must admit I had my season of doubt. I had experienced sickness, been the target of muggers several times (though praise God they never got anything off of me) and like many a volunteer, I had a real sense of disillusionment with my job in the first year. I had great expectations of how I might be able to be of assistance in my professional niche, but the reality was that I didn't make much of an impact. I wasn't bringing water to a village or starting a co-op. I was an extra hand in a juvenile detention facility. That's not to say I had no impact, it just wasn't as significant as I had imagined it might be. Turns out that my mid-career Ecuadorian counterparts were not as eager to learn from an American kid right out of college as I was eager to teach them!

One of my greatest challenges in the Peace Corps, however, was not job-related at all. It was housing. After three months with a host family, I rented a third floor of a house; it was the roof really, but it had two enclosed rooms and a bathroom and the price was right. One night upon returning home from a weekend away, I walked up the stairs and saw what looked like snow covering everything I owned. I opened the bedroom and the snow was covering the floor and my bed. I walked into the kitchen and found all my dishes, silverware and cookware covered in snow. The only things that hadn't been snowed on were the clothes in my closet. The snow was actually dust. That weekend, workmen had been in the house to sand down the wooden floors on the first and second stories to prepare them for refinishing. The wood and old varnish had drifted upstairs and into everything but my clothes.

It took me a couple of hours just to be able to create a place for sleeping – I only had one set of sheets, and I did laundry by hand in a huge cement water tank with a washboard, so washing my sheets that night wasn't an option. I didn't rest very well that night and the entire next two days I spent dusting – although it seems more correct to say undusting – everything.

A week or so later, I was at work and the strangest thing happened. I starting seeing a transparent spot in my vision – that's the best way I can describe it. It was just in one corner of my vision. That lasted about 15 minutes and then I began to feel weak, so weak in fact that I picked my things up immediately and went to get on a bus to go home. I lived about 30 minutes away from work and was wondering if I would make it.

When I got to the bus stop in front of the Peace Corps office, I got off and went to visit the nurses. I collapsed on their cot with the most massive headache I've ever had. They gave me 800 mg. of ibuprofen and I slept there for two hours. When I woke up, my head was still in a vice grip, but I left for home. I slept the rest of the day at home and woke up that evening in a fog. The next morning I felt normal. I had no idea what hit me, and I later learned it was a migraine headache – my first.

Through some testing, I learned that I had a severe allergy to dust, probably from overexposure. Go figure. I had several more migraines at inconvenient times and those were completely wasted days for me, spent in agonizing pain, as anyone who has migraines can tell you. I went through an allergy desensitization treatment, a shot a week for 44 weeks, and praise God, it worked; I don't suffer from migraines anymore.

That dusty experience really soured me on the landlord of my roof-top abode, and I moved out a few weeks later. When the day I was supposed to move came, I didn't have a place to go. It was hard finding a good, cheap place to live in Ecuador's capital city of Quito. A friend offered to let me housesit with him for a month and that gave me more time to find a place. The place I found was great and had only one drawback: I had to share a bathroom. But I loved the fireplace and garden space of my apartment.

After I'd been in my new place one month, the sheriff came and posted an eviction notice on my door. Turns out the person who had rented me the apartment was not the owner of the house. She was subletting it to me and she hadn't paid the rent, not just my rent, but the rent of everyone in the large house – about five of us. The real owner didn't want a bunch of people living in his house anyway, so he wouldn't rent directly to us. He wanted us out.

The woman who rented to me wouldn't return the money I had just paid nor my deposit. I was out of money and in desperate need to find a place to live in 24 hours in a city that had precious little safe, affordable housing for singles. Both as the straw that broke the camel's back and a blessing in disguise, this eviction notice arrived during the visit of the only relative who came to visit me during my Peace Corps service – my 74-year-old grandmother. I probably could have handled living out of box with my two cats for a while, but what about Grandma? But thank God for Grandma, she was a shoulder to cry on – and I did, like a baby!

Grandma went to stay with an American family who lived in Quito on a military exchange program and I found a place that some departing volunteers were vacating. I didn't really like it or the landlady who lived on site, but it was a stable place to live, and I ended up staying there for a year.

Through all of this, and more that I haven't detailed, I remember leaning against the kitchen doorway in that final apartment thinking to myself, "Why am I doing this? What is keeping me here?" Except for saying good-bye to my cats, it would have been so easy to just resign and be on a plane heading for home two days later. There was no penalty for quitting. So what, I couldn't put Peace Corps on my resume; that hardly seemed a deterrent compared to all the hassle that just living and finding a place to live in Ecuador had become.

I was sick of it all, and in that moment, all the things I couldn't stand about the experience aggregated and felt overwhelming. The staticy radio reception on the buses – why couldn't the driver tune into a station! The intestinal parasites – I was ready to eat a piece of fruit without bleaching it first! The constant barrage of glares and hisses that any somewhat attractive young *gringa* is subjected to as she walks down the street – I wanted to slap the face of every Ecuadorian man! I was not a happy camper. I know how so many of the others came to the place where they evaluated that it was not worth it to stick it out.

I really can't say why I didn't quit. Besides the cats, there was nothing keeping me there. But I said to myself, "I will hold out for a few months more. If I still feel this way in three months, I'll go home."

Three months went by. I still had problems – radio static, parasites and shameless men – throughout my Peace Corps service. My job never really got any better and I ended up moving yet again, but I never flirted with the idea of going home again like I had that day. That was my lowest point and that's never a good time to give up. After all, it's all uphill from the lowest point.

It's not possible to know when we've hit bottom, but when it feels like bottom and we feel ready to throw in the towel, that's a good sign we're at the bottom. That's the time to hold on. That's the time to say, "I will not make a decision in this state; I will wait

It's not possible to know when we've hit bottom, but when it feels like bottom and we feel ready to throw in the towel, that's a good sign we're at the bottom. That's the time to hold on.

three months more" (or three hours, days or weeks, depending on the circumstances). This ensures that we are not making decisions out of the weakness of our emotional despair and instead, we are making well-thought out, carefully planned decisions. In that waiting time, we may find ourselves preparing to quit – planning our next move, finding something better to go on to. Or, like I did in the Peace Corps, we may find ourselves adjusting and learning to ignore the negative and focus on the positive about our current situation, realizing that this too will pass. Either way, we'll be making a decision based on strength of character, not emotional weakness.

Hold this thought: When I'm ready to quit, I'll flex some mental muscle and hold on for a little longer.

Keep an Eye out for Snakes
and Other Distortions of Reality

What you have seen with your eyes do not bring hastily to court, for what will you do in the end if your neighbor puts you to shame?
Proverbs 25:8

You've probably read in a science or psychology book that the human brain filters information. It has to. All of our senses are taking in infinite detail at all moments, yes, even in our sleep. According to some scientists, we're recording it all. But we never know it because our brain has to be very picky about what we pay attention to or else we would crash from sensory overload. Sound crazy? Check it out (see the bibliography).

A lot of how the brain filters information has to do with our safety and security. If anything comes into contact with our senses that our brain perceives to be a threat, our attention is immediately drawn to it. Like the eight-inch earthworm I saw while I was walking today. I really wasn't looking down or any-where in particular, that I can recall. Just as I stepped over the earthworm, it wiggled (probably freaking out over my threat-ening presence) and I spotted it. Nothing draws my attention as effectively as a long, slimy creature on the ground. Why? Because I'm afraid of snakes. I used to have a textbook phobia of them but have progressed to the point where after the ini-tial startle of happening upon one, I can watch calmly as my husband does battle with it to catch and release it somewhere a mile or so down the road. It's the lucky ones that take a ride in the truck. The uncooperative or slit-eye variety meet with a tragic end.

Though snakes, the poisonous ones at least, can be a threat to all humans, not every person's filters are set to pick up on a snake on the ground. A few months ago, my husband and I were hiking in the early spring. He was leading the way keeping an eye out for snakes – a gallant service he lovingly provides as he is not really afraid of snakes (though he startles at first sight too). Even though he led, I had my eyes on the leaf-strewn ground anyway, as an extra precaution. Well, you guessed it, he stepped right over a snake without any inkling. The same slithery sucker caught my attention in a big way and I let out one of my famous ultrasonic squeals! That's not the first time that has happened either – and not just with my husband but with others I've hiked with too.

242

Why do I always see the snakes? My sister says it's because I'm looking for them. And you know that's so true – I have my filters programmed to block out rare mosses and lichens and attend to the slithery things in my path.

Now that you see how this works, it's easy to understand how our preprogrammed information filters can cause us not only to attend to specific things that others don't see, but they can cause us to interpret information in certain ways. Often those ways don't correspond to reality.

The essence of this proverb is that often when we think we have things figured out, we don't. There are two main things getting in the way of our truly understanding matters like we think we do. The first is incomplete information. Even when the situation involves a family member, best friend or roommate, who we think we know so well, there's always something they are not telling us, which if we knew, would shed a new light on things. The second limiting factor is our own personal filters.

When I was the director of Hope House, I hired a weekend house parent who only worked for a short time – it just didn't work out for her. In that time, however, she and I became friends. We had a few key things in common – we were both single mothers, she was homeschooling her son and I hoped to homeschool my daughter when she became school age. Although she was from Washington, a state I've never even visited, I felt like we shared similar perspectives more so than I did with my fellow southerners. I liked this gal. I visited her home; she visited mine. She babysat for me when I had evening meetings. It seemed like a solid friendship was emerging. Then one day I called to ask if she could watch my daughter but she didn't answer the phone. I left a message. She didn't call back. The occasion passed. I called again just to say "hi." She didn't answer. I left a message. She didn't call back. Over a period of about a month, that same scenario played out a couple of times more. She was blowing me off! After some careful thought about what might have gone wrong, I finally decided that I had abused the friendship by asking her one too many times to watch my daughter. She never asked me to babysit, in fact, I didn't do anything to return her favors to me. I had blown it. I felt bad about it and also felt a little rejected – she didn't like me enough to hang in there or just tell me she didn't want to babysit so much.

243

Then one day about three months later, she called. The first thing out of her mouth was an apology for having been incommunicado for so long. The next thing was the real reason why: she was pregnant. She was 30 years old, never married, had one child out of wedlock and was now pregnant with another – by another man. To have this happen once was humiliating – for it to happen again made her have to face some hard reality about herself and she didn't like what she saw. And then there was the concern over how she would provide for another child when she was barely making ends meet with the one she had. She had decided to move back to Washington and live near her mother to get some help. This was what was wrong, not that I had asked her one too many times to baby-sit or that she had not liked me enough.

That experience taught me a lot about my own filters and jumping to conclusions based on incomplete information. I think a lot of people are like me in that we take things more personally than we should. In fact, not everything is about me! I have learned to notice when I am filtering information through the "it's about me" filter, and go through the important mental exercise of concocting several other scenarios that could explain what I'm seeing.

When the neighbor speeds by me on the road near our house without waving, I begin to think of some reasons why she might not have even noticed my presence. Maybe she's calculating bills in her head and feeling a little overwhelmed by the sum. Maybe she's late to pick up her kids and is kicking herself for having, once again, piddled around too long before leaving. Maybe she just caught her husband looking at porn! There could be a hundred different reasons why she's not attending to who's passing her on the road – even something as simple as maybe the sun is in her eyes!

We need to slow down before we make assumptions, examine our own filters, try to diffuse them and consider other possibilities. We should seek more information, and if that's not possible, play out some other plausible explanations for what we're seeing. It could save us the mental angst and humiliation that often accompany incorrect assumptions.

Hold this thought: Maybe there's another explanation.

Time to Buy a New Car, God Willing

Do not boast about tomorrow, for you do not know what a day may bring forth.

Proverbs 27:1

Do you know someone who's always saying, "God willing," as a caveat to all their plans? Some people do it out of habit, others out of the sincere acknowledgement that God must allow us to do everything we actually do. Honestly, that phrase can get annoying, but it indicates a mature perspective. I don't think it's necessary to say "God willing" twenty times a day – "I'm going to bathroom now, God willing," "Hey, let's go eat, God willing," – but it is necessary to remain constantly cognizant of God's omnipotence and ability to change our plans and even our lives in a moment.

There are a googol ways our plans can change unexpectedly and out of our control. I had a plan to keep my Cadillac Catera for a total of eight years (I bought it used). I thought if I maintained it well, it would surely last that long. After five years and I began to doubt the car would make it to eight years. Despite my careful efforts at preventive maintenance, I had no idea that my husband would hit a deer on Monday, December 11. And then imagine my surprise when the following year, I hit a deer on Monday, December 12.

The car was totaled by the insurance company and I had a decision to make. Take the cash the insurance company was going to give me, get the car fixed and keeping driving it, just without comprehensive insurance coverage, or take the cash and invest in a new car. I decided to stick with my plan to make the Cadillac last eight years and I got the car fixed. I felt pretty good about sticking to my plan until a couple of months later, when the transmission started to slip. I took the car to a transmission shop and they told me it would cost $2,200 to fix the cheap way. They also told me I could continue to drive the car using a manual shifting method. So I did that and revised my plan to include a new car much sooner.

Then one day, the transmission didn't malfunction. I thought it was a fluke, but day after day after day it continued to behave itself. My car was healed! It took a couple of months to believe it, but when I finally was convinced, I changed my plan to keep the car again, like I had originally planned.

Then another day, the car didn't start. The battery seemed dead. Upon further investigation, it seemed the alternator was the problem. The mechanic said it was a $400 job (everything is more expensive with a Cadillac). So we began the new car search again. A month passed from that day the car wouldn't start, and though the voltage didn't seem to be climbing as high as it should, the car was running just fine. What to do: Buy a new car or wait to see how much longer the Cadillac would last? At that point, I figuratively shredded any plans I had about keeping or ditching the car. I was officially flying by the seat of my pants.

During the whole auto ordeal, between my husband, my daughter and me, we probably boasted a dozen times that we were getting a new car. When the transmission was on the fritz, it seemed certain, then it didn't, then with the alternator, it seemed certain again, and then it didn't again. People were probably wondering when the Schillingers were going to get that new car they kept talking about.

That car situation really

> I had no idea that my husband would hit a deer on Monday, December 11. And then imagine my surprise when the following year, I hit a deer on Monday, December 12.

kept me guessing, planning and revising my plan – it was a good lesson in living day by day, trusting God and refraining from trying to be my own fortune teller.

Hold this thought: Bragging about future plans is as good as an invitation to have them changed.

P. S. In case you're wondering, before it conked out, we traded the Caddy in on a one-year-old Honda Element – that "new field" I mentioned in the section about budgeting.

247

chapter ten

This is Me – Fearless!

Taps for Todd

Young and Foolish

The Last Scary Movie I Saw Was the Last I'll Ever See

Say His Name, Say His Name

A Charmed Life

Is the World Spinning out of Control?

Taps for Todd

He holds victory in store for the upright, he is a shield to those whose walk is blameless, for he guards the course of the just and protects the way of his faithful ones.

Proverbs 2:7-8

I really like these two verses for the promises they pack: victory, a shield, a guard and protection. I almost feel invincible! And that's good because the world is a scary place. There are natural disasters, dangerous natural phenomenon, animals that can hurt us and the most frightening of all – evil men.

What do evil men look like? Are they ugly with twisted faces? Are they poor and homeless? If we could tell evil men by the way they look, it would be fairly easy to steer clear of them. Evil men come in all shapes and sizes. Some wear Armani, some wear Levis, some have manicured nails, and some don't own a brush. There are no criteria for spotting an evil man. It's not easy to tell one by the way he acts either. Some evil men seem really nice, even for a long time.

When I was a sophomore in high school, I really liked a trumpet player named Todd. We went to school together every day and I saw how he behaved; he was a good student, clean-cut and had a nice car. I didn't know anything about his family, but thought he must be a pretty good guy if he made good grades and was in the band. I tried to flirt with Todd, but I was shy and not too good at it. I sent word through the grapevine that I liked him. One day, he offered my friend and me a ride home from school. Was romance about to blossom? I was so hopeful.

Not long after, Todd called me one day after school. I was so nervous, my hands were shaky and I was pacing around my room while I tried to think of something clever to say. He must be calling to ask me out, I thought. We talked for just a couple of minutes and then his tone of voice changed. He started sounding sleepy and sick but what he was saying revealed other feelings. He was talking dirty to me – very dirty. Fortunately, the shock of what was happening stunned my long-term memory. I can't recall anything he said and I am so grateful for that. I just remember it was very vulgar. He was an evil young man. As soon as I gained sufficient composure, I hung up on him. Then I called my friends and told them what a jerk he was.

250   I am glad I never got the date with him for which I so wished. It was one of the first of many times I can vividly recall that God shielded me, guarded me and protected me from evil. I made a wise choice to hang up and have nothing more to do with Todd, and although I was disillusioned and somewhat embarrassed, I was not harmed. In fact, I was wiser for that experience. About five years later, Todd died in a car accident. I hope he had a change of heart before his accident.

Hold this thought: God is guarding and protecting me.

Young and Foolish

Wisdom will save you from the ways of wicked men, from men whose words are perverse, who leave the straight paths to walk in dark ways, who delight in doing wrong and rejoice in the perverseness of evil, whose paths are crooked and who are devious in their ways.

Proverbs 2:12-15

Todd's crank call was a learning experience, but I didn't learn enough about evil men from that lesson. Specifically, I didn't learn the point I am trying to make – that you can't tell an evil man by the way he looks. It wasn't just ignorance of that fact that got me into big trouble one day. If wisdom will save you from the ways of wicked men, consider the result abandoning wisdom might have.

A wise person protects herself. She keeps her car door locked; she locks her house door at night; she sleeps with her accessible windows closed. She doesn't walk alone at night and avoids walking alone even in the daytime if possible. A wise person is not afraid, she is careful. She stays on the path of prudence. A wise person would never hitchhike.

Though hitchhiking could be a necessity some day if you find yourself stranded a long way away from the nearest phone, it's a very risky, imprudent behavior. Generally speaking, the kind of people who hitchhike and the kind who pick up hitchhikers are people with nothing to lose in life. They don't care if they are putting the life God gave them at risk. I hope you never feel that way and I hope you never hitchhike.

Hitchhiking in Europe in the last century was not as dangerous as it is today, but the fact of the matter is that hitchhiking anywhere at any time in history has always held an element of risk – one that a wise person will avoid with better planning.

With that said, I'd like to tell you about a dangerous encounter I had with an evil man during a time in my life that I had abandoned wisdom.

A friend and I had hitchhiked from Spain across Portugal to a major city on the coast, Port. On the outskirts of the city, we enjoyed the black-sanded beaches and a typical Saturday in Portugal. After a game of checkers in a local haunt, it was time to find a hostel in which to stay the night. We had a one-mile walk back into the business district of the closest town.

As we were walking, a car slowed down and a nice-looking young man asked us if we needed a ride. We didn't really, but having just successfully hitchhiked across a country, we were feeling rather secure about getting into cars with strangers – a false security. We accepted the ride. We communicated in our Spanish to his Portuguese that we wanted to find a place to stay the night. He made some suggestions and then asked if we had seen the windmills. No, we hadn't. Well, he would take us to see the windmills first, then to find a hotel room, or we could even stay with him if we liked. At this point, you can probably see something is amiss. But believe it or not, my friend and I still had no inkling this guy was a creep.

He took us high on a mountain to see the historic Dutch-style windmills and a beautiful vista of the area. There were a lot of people there – it was a tourist spot. But the route to get there was largely through sparsely inhabited woods.

When we were ready to go, the driver pulled the car up and I got in first – into the back seat – and as soon as I did, he took off. What about my friend? He told me we would come back for her as soon as he and I made love. On the outside I stayed calm as I began to inwardly panic. I was in the back seat of a two-door car, so I could not jump out. What to do?

He drove about half-way down the mountain and turned down a side road into the woods. He got in the back seat with

252

me. I was trying every way I could think of to talk him out of what he had in mind. I told him I had AIDS. He told me he had a gun. Here I was, smack dab in the path of an evil man. I had left the path of wisdom and started walking on a path where I could find just such a man. Was I happy now that I had saved $50 on train fare by hitchhiking? Was I happy now this guy had saved me a one-mile walk?

As he was undressing, I saw my opportunity, coiled my legs and then let them spring into his midsection. The moment that he needed to recover was enough time for me to nudge past him and out the door. I ran hard and fast for a long time and did not look back.

253

I finally came across a home with a rustic wooden fence. I jumped the fence and went around the back of the house full speed until I saw a German shepherd. Barking wildly, it charged me, but it was chained so I continued toward the house just out of its reach. The back door was open and lights were on inside. I went in saying "*Hola*," quite loudly. There didn't seem to be anyone there. I still had the frantic feeling I was being chased, so I worked my way through the house until I came to a dead end. I slipped into a closet and squatted down in the dark and waited. I have never been more scared in my life than I was then, hunkered down in that dark closet of a stranger's house in Po-dunk, Portugal. I don't know how long I was there.

When I heard a woman's voice, I crept out of the closet. It's almost funny now to recall the expression of shock and terror on this young mother's face as she saw this tall Caucasian woman emerging from her bedroom. With baby in arms, she turned tail and ran out of the house. I figured she would be back so I waited on the back porch until she returned with about 20 people, including one off-duty police officer who helped me eventually reunite with my traveling partner.

That experience changed the way I looked at life. A basic

trust I held in people was damaged. I shudder to think how my life could have changed had that nice-looking, evil man carried out his plan. God saved me from a lot worse that day – despite my foolishness. I am so thankful that He did not abandon me like I had abandoned wisdom.

My friend and I took the train back to Spain. We had learned that lesson, but unfortunately, were still pretty foolish girls. When the train stopped at the Spanish/Portuguese border for dinner, in some way I still can't understand, my friend and I miscalculated the train departure time and it left without us. No other trains were coming that night. A conductor told us that the train would be stopping for a few minutes on the Spanish side, if we ran following the tracks, we might catch it. My friend may have stood a chance, but I have never been a runner. About half a mile down the tracks, I was huffing and cramping (especially after having just eaten dinner!). We watched in desperation as the train within our view, but not our grasp, pulled away from the Spanish side leaving us behind.

What were we to do? There was no town nearby and we didn't have any money even if there had been a place to stay – we spent our last dime on dinner. Can you guess what we did? We hitched a ride with a trucker. No comment.

Hold this thought: I must not abandon wisdom for adventure.

The Last Scary Movie I Saw
Was the Last I'll Ever See

My daughter, preserve sound judgment and discernment, do not let them out of your sight; they will be life for you, an ornament to grace your neck. Then you will go on your way in safety, and your foot will not stumble; when you lie down, you will not be afraid; when you lie down, your sleep will be sweet. Have no fear of sudden disaster or of the ruin that overtakes the wicked, for the Lord will be your confidence and will keep your foot from being snared.

Proverbs 3:21-26

I said it before, I'll say it again: the world is a scary place – weirdos doing bizarre things and so much violence. And the architect of it all is Satan. Even if we never encounter evil face to face, contemplating the diversity of psychosis in this world can make us feel abnormal for being sane. It can also cause our minds to spin out endless scenarios of how the evil of the world could reach us.

Fear is a God-given emotion and is quite healthy for us in real, scary situations. Fear can transform our bodies, giving them extraordinary abilities. It is a natural high. Thanks to the safety of our homes and society, most of us don't have to feel fear in life. But because of the natural high it gives, people seek out fear in artificial situations. Riding a gnarly roller coaster will give that fear-induced high. And if you have a desire to get that high, that is exactly what I would recommend.

Much more common and less expensive is the fear-induced high that comes from watching horror movies or reading horror novels. The real world is enough to keep a person awake at night with fear; add to that the negative fantasy of books, movies and television and it is a wonder anyone sleeps well at night. Whereas a roller coaster ride is not likely to haunt us for days, weeks, months to come, after we see a horror film, we may feel fear for a long time. We get our fear-induced high while we watch the movie, but that's not all. We are left with a residual of fear that takes a long time to work out of our system. It's fantasy fear, but it feels real.

When I was 12 years old, I visited my Great Aunt Yutha who lived in Michigan. I stayed up late one night to watch a vampire movie. That night, in the upstairs bedroom of my unfamiliar surroundings, I had such an intense (and illogical) fear of vampires that I fell asleep with my hands clasped around my neck and my fingers in the shape of a cross. When I woke up the next morning, I realized how inane my fear had been. Watching a movie about vampires does not make them real and even if they are real, it doesn't put me at any greater risk of being attacked by one. But logic is ineffective against fear, which is one thing that makes fear so destructive.

The real harm that negative film and fantasy books do is to rob us of our peace of mind. They produce an unsubstantiated fear that runs in the background of our mind and undermines our abundant life as independent women. The fact of the matter is that women are more at risk of being victims of grotesque crimes than men. And that simple statistic, along with the garbage of negative fantasy, can zap us of the courage we need to do safe, simple things like go into our own basement or attic.

All the negative influences of the world, fantasy and real, can cripple us with fear. But we do not have to live that way. As single women in this world, we can do anything we want – think of how small and fragile Mother Theresa was and yet she lived in places most burly American men would fear going alone.

What's needed is sound judgment and discernment to take proactive, cautious measures to protect ourselves. Pro-action based on sound judgment feels very different than re-action to protect ourselves, based on fear. For example, we should be in the proactive habit of locking our doors at night. When that time comes, we make the rounds through the house, securing doors and windows and then calmly retire. That same routine can be performed as a reaction to fear and the big difference is that we don't feel calm and confident as we're locking the doors. Instead we feel panic and fear – like there's a boogey man just on the other side of that door and if we don't get it locked in time, he may come bursting through.

"God has not given us a spirit of fear, but of power, and of love and a sound mind" (II Timothy 1:7). When we have a problem with fear, we need to detox our minds as a first step to free ourselves from fear's grip over our lives. We cannot remove the material we've already taken in, but time will weaken those images eventually to the point they no longer influence us. We can start today to protect our minds by not watching any more horror shows and not reading horror novels. This is a small sacrifice to gain freedom from fear and all the independence that courage enables – not to mention the sweet sleep.

Hold this thought: I won't watch scary movies anymore.

Say His Name, Say His Name

The name of the Lord is a strong tower; the righteous run to it and are safe.

Proverbs 18:10

With all the wonderful promises in the Bible, it's tempting to believe if we will only live in the center of God's will, we can go through life unscathed. Yet it seems that there is a measure of trauma for every life – even the most brief. If we would examine the lives of the men who penned the divine promises, we'd see their lives were marked with adversity. Almost every great Bible story has a strong element of adversity. So, please, if you live under the delusion that you may be "charmed" because no one in your family has ever died and you've had it pretty easy thus far, begin now to prepare yourself mentally for the inevitable.

And here's how: We must learn to keep our eyes on Jesus and call out His name in our times of trouble. If all we have is minor troubles now, we should use this strategy anyway so that it will be a familiar response for when the major ones come along.

In our darkest hour, we may feel alone for long stretches of time. Whatever the situation that put us in that place, even if there is no element of evil, Satan will take advantage of this time to attack. He's cunning and wouldn't let such an opportunity pass. Satan will cause us to doubt our sanity, wonder if life is worth living, have auditory or visual hallucinations and use any number of guerilla tactics. When this happens, we've got to pull ourselves together in two steps. First, recognize this for what it is. Secondly, disarm it with the name of Jesus. In that name we will be safe – even if we are not actually physically safe.

Remember the story of the disciples struggling to keep control of their boat on the lake during a storm? They looked out into the wind and waves and saw what looked like a ghost walking on the water. It was Jesus and He called out, identifying Himself.

Peter said, "Lord, if it's really you, tell me to come to you on the water." So Jesus said, "Come."

That doesn't sound to me like such a great way to confirm someone's identity, but it was enough for Peter and he stepped out of the boat – with his eyes fixed on Jesus – and started walking on water, as Jesus was doing. Then, he looked down and around and remembered the wind and the waves and realized he was standing on water, which is a physical impossibility. He started to sink. Then he cried out again, "Lord, save me." Jesus immediately reached out His hand and pulled Peter up and they both got back in the boat (Matthew 14:22-33).

259

I love that story because it is a great allegory for every trial in life. Even when we have the faith to enter the trial with our eyes on Jesus, it seems the storm distracts us; we can't help but look around at the mess we're in and start to panic. If we will then call on Jesus, He's faithful to reach out His hand and see us through the trial, all the way until we're back into the boat and the storm is over.

Notice in the story, it says that Jesus *immediately* reached out His hand. I believe it's impossible to be focusing on Jesus with your full attention and be afraid at the same time. When we experience fear, whether from life's trauma or because we just heard something go bump in the night and we can't figure out

Please, if you live under the delusion that you may be "charmed" because no one in your family has ever died and you've had it pretty easy thus far, begin now to prepare yourself mentally for the inevitable.

what it might be, if we will focus our full attention on calling on the Lord, our fear will fade immediately – that's how quick Jesus will reach out to us. Don't be surprised to find that when we lose focus on Jesus, we start to feel fear again. So focus again on God – this takes some mental discipline. With enough focus, our adversary, who is not whatever real or imagined person or event precipitated the fear, but Satan himself, will go back to hell because we're obviously not buying what he's selling.

This works. I know it sounds crazy now, but it will look pretty appealing next time you have a good scare.

Hold this thought: When I feel fear, I will call on Jesus.

A Charmed Life

Do not let your heart envy sinners, but always be zealous for the fear of the Lord. There is surely a future hope for you and your hope will not be cut off.

Proverbs 23:17-18

Okay, so we know there's no such thing as a charmed life. But what about those people for whom everything seems to go their way? When those people are Christians, we may think they are blessed by God. But what about unbelievers whose lives seem perfect? In fact, I could probably name more unbelievers who seem to have blessed lives than believers. I confess that I have looked at people to my left and to my right and wondered, "Why does everything go right for them?"

That's an outsider's observation and I bet some people used to ask it of me. And indeed for about 30 years, despite a lot of crap around me, I seemed to be able to cut through it all and always float to the top. That charmed life I led was a function of not having lived very long. Because eventually major trials came my way and now, it's impossible to know very much about me and conclude that I've lived a charmed life. I still seem to rise to the top of flotsam around me, but because of two very sobering events, no one would ever mistake me for having a charmed life: I became pregnant outside of marriage, spending more than six years as a single mother, and my second child died at birth – two events that challenged my hold on hope.

I'm convinced that if we live long enough, at least once in every life there is a test of our ability to remain hopeful – a personal tragedy. And if we don't live long enough, well, that would be the personal tragedy in itself. The test seems to be one of the requirements for graduation from life. It's a huge waste of energy to worry about what ours might be or try to prevent it.

The one important thing we can be doing now is to strengthen our character so that when that event arrives, it doesn't do us in completely or rob us of our hope. We need to have the fortitude to trudge through the muck of tragedy to the other side, where we'll find hope waiting.

Sadly, some people flunk the test of regaining hope after tragedy. Some of those that fail take their own lives; others remain living as though they were dead already. Still others seem to have bounced back but underneath a fairly normal exterior is fear and mistrust that cripples them from taking risks in career, relationships and faith. Then there are those who find hope again, latch on to it and this time have a much stronger grip.

When we survive a tragedy and find hope again, we have an incredible security about our hold on hope. We have taken some of the worst things life has to dish out and bounced back! We know, in a way that was not possible to know prior to our personal experience with tragedy, that we have a future hope, and like north on a compass, it's always there. No matter what happens in life, when the storms of life pick us up, twirl us around and throw us back down somewhere way off of our previous course, if we persevere in seeking, we will find "north" again.

Perseverance is simply hoping when we don't feel hopeful. When hope has been yanked out of our hands, perseverance is the light residue that our former hope left behind. We don't feel hope anymore, we don't believe, but if we will just refuse to give up, that remnant of hope left on us will guide us to the mother lode again.

After my son passed away, I didn't feel any hope. I had a reason to live – I had my daughter – but that was all I felt like I was living for, not out of any will of my own, but just so she would not suffer any more. And that's what got me out of bed in the morning and reinstated a routine in our household. For a while, I didn't think I'd ever laugh again or be happy again. Every smile felt forced and false and when I heard myself laughing, it sounded like someone else. The tragedy was so disorienting that I could not recognize anything of my previous self!

I was hurt, and because I knew God was in control, I didn't feel too kindly toward God or put much stock in God's promises. I was so confused. I can easily see how tragedy causes some people to completely lose their bearings in life.

Praise God, I found "north" again through a journey I've chronicled in *Dear Hunter*. It's a free e-book available at www.OnMyOwnNow.com.

God's love is a search and rescue party in our time of trouble – it's out there looking for us. We must hang on. God will bring us back.

Hold this thought: I will hope again, if I just hold on.

Is the World Spinning out of Control?

There is no wisdom, no insight, no plan that can succeed against the Lord. The horse is made ready for the day of battle but victory rests with the Lord.

Proverbs 21:30-31

264

My neighbor is studying to become a nurse. One semester, she took a class called Death and Dying. For a final project, she had to do an oral presentation on mothers who kill their babies. She came to my house to print her presentation because she couldn't get her printer to work. While she worked, she shared some of what she had learned about mothers who kill their children.

In the United States, the number one cause of death of children under four is murder by a primary caregiver and over 200 children die at their mother's hand each year.

This was hard to believe since I can only recall a couple of high-profile cases of this sort of atrocity, although there does seem to be another newborn found in a dumpster somewhere every couple of months, which might get a brief mention in the news. But as it turns out, several children will die today – murdered by their mother, grandmother, aunt, uncle, sister, father – someone left in charge of caring for them. And then tomorrow, it will happen again and the day after that, several more will die. And apparently this barely reported nightmare has stayed somewhat constant and proportionately steady throughout its recorded history of several centuries.

Why is America not obsessing over the murder of each child the way we did over the Andrea Yates case? You might not even remember that. It happened in 2001; a depressed woman drowned her five children. That is the last high-profile murder-by-mother case I remember. If the media gave equal attention to every child's murder, it would create a public outrage sufficient to drive our society to do something to drastically reduce the child murder rates. One bill currently under consideration would allow a mother a certain grace period after giving birth to drop her child at any hospital or police station, sign a paper and be rid of her parental responsibility for good. Sounds awful, but is clearly preferable to that same mother becoming so desperately frustrated that she kills her child.

My neighbor, a loving mother of four, was quite disturbed by all she had discovered, impassioned against it and maybe even somewhat temporarily obsessed by it. She read of one case study where a young mother had stabbed her six-pound baby over 120 times. My neighbor said she reenacted the stabbing action the full count and with each downward stroke became more and more incredulous that any person, even an obviously insane person, could do such a thing.

265

My neighbor was rightly disturbed. I hadn't done her extensive research – I was greatly disturbed just on the second-hand report! I talked to my husband about it and later, some friends and now I'm writing about it. I'm using it as the example of the most disconcerting thing I can think of. To me, these crimes against the most innocent should be more alarming than terrorist attacks – and they have certainly killed more people.

So what's a person to do about it? I pondered that for a long time. And I wonder that about a lot of other things too. There's no dearth of current events to obsess over. Gas prices, global warming, mercury-poisoned fish, destruction of the rain forest, racial and ethnic genocide, the confounding Electoral College! Take your pick! It all seems so completely out of control. My blood pressure spiked just penning that list!

They say ignorance is bliss and I believe it. I'm not advocating being completely uninformed, but I do believe that we can overindulge on media coverage about current events and end up all in a tizzy with no way to unwind. This is the primary reason I don't watch, read or listen to a daily news report. Before you think that sounds like a cop out, let me say that I used to be a religious reader of *Newsweek* – cover to cover, baby, every week. Sure, I knew a lot more about a lot more, but what did all that knowledge do for me? In the final analysis, I wasn't benefiting from being informed because, although I might have been a better conversationalist, I was perpetually disturbed.

As we examine the world's insanity, we can't help but feel a little desperate, or worse, we grow calloused. Of the two, I'd rather feel disturbed – it's a natural human reaction and it's productive. Our discomfort compels us to want to make the world a better place. Before mass media, a person's glimpse of the world's insanity was limited to craziness in close proximity. Now, however, there seems to be no end to the insanity. If it's a slow news day in our country, the media can look to Indonesia or Chad or Surinam or anywhere to get its shocking story that sells. The result is an unnatural balance of exposure to insanity and an excess of the desperate emotions it provokes in us. If you are like me, sensitive to bad news, I highly recommend you limit your intake of news to a monthly magazine that will keep you informed by reporting on the big issues in a comprehensive way and won't bog you down with constant bad news hype that can disturb your daily peace. That monthly magazine will disturb you enough.

So what do we do with all that emotional disturbance? Well, we should turn it into positive action. If we don't have some outlet in our life to effect positive societal or world change, we have no way to channel all those emotions out of our system. They will become toxic sludge inside us. We need to find a cause we can support and as we're engaged in it, release (let go of) the emotions the world's insanity has stirred in us.

That takes care of us, but what about the world? It's still insane! No, it's not. (Who said that? Now, I'm arguing with myself? Help!)

There is insanity in the world, but the world is not insane, it's not spinning out of control, it's not on a course for self-destruction and a meteor is not going to come along some day and knock the earth out of the sky. How do I know all of this? It's in God's word – even the part about the meteor. Psalms 104:5 says, "He set the earth on its foundation; it can never be moved." And if you know the rest of the story, you know God has great plans for the earth – the physical globe and everything on it is completely under God's control, every waking and sleeping moment.

The tabloids poke fun at prophecies, and I agree that some people take it to the extreme. Seems one church has predicted Christ's return incorrectly about ten times now. We can really get bogged down in the signs and prophecies about the end of time as we know it, but we needn't do that. It's enough to accept that every single movement, even on the molecular level, is happening as God allows. No wisdom, no insight, no plan can counter God. This does not mean it is God's will for mothers to kill their babies. Sin happens and it's not God's will. Yet this Master Logistician can take all the failings of our humanity and work them to His glory.

God already knows the resolution to all the world's problems and all our individual problems. God is in control. In fact, some of the very things we may be fighting so hard to change could be an integral part of God's plan.

Hold this thought: The world seems crazy, but God is in control.

chapter eleven

Taking It to the Next Level

You've Got the Makings of a Mighty Woman of God

As Essential as Underwear

268

Tell Me if You Know!

Something to Shoot For

You've Got the Makings of a Mighty Woman of God

It is not for kings, O Lemuel – not for kings to drink wine, not for rulers to crave beer … Give beer to those who are perishing, wine to those who are in anguish; let them drink and forget their poverty and remember their misery no more.

Proverbs 31:4, 6

If you've come this far with me, I must say you are something special. A lot of young women will receive this book as a gift or buy it for themselves and never make it to this page. Unless you skipped ahead, the fact that you're reading this now says something very complimentary about you. You care about your future enough to invest time and energy in seeking counsel and understanding of God's word. You are on the road to becoming a mighty woman of God. What can stand in your way? Glad you asked…

As we learn from King Lemuel's mother, worldly appetites can stand in the way of us becoming mighty women of God – a queen in our own right, a ruler. Say you don't drink? Great. Don't start and you'll never have to overcome a craving for it. Wine and beer in this verse are, however, simply examples of the many appetites of the flesh that drag us down. Here are some others:

- Secular music – particularly music with lyrics about sex, depressing love songs and even so-called empowering songs that bombard us with egoistic messages like, "It's my life."

- Television and movies – basically everything on network television in the 9 p.m. prime-time spot is garbage, but even the lighter shows earlier in the evening are riddled with cultural messages that run contrary to the holy life we need to live to be mighty women of God. And if the shows don't get us, the commercials will. But the worst thing about television and movies too – even the good ones – is that if we're not careful, we can spend so much time watching them that we edge out time for the kind of things that will advance us in life.

- Books – My beloved books? Yes, even books can be an appetite of the flesh. What kind of books are we reading? Do we learn useful information from them? Do they inspire us? Are they filled with positive ideas? That sounds like a good use of time. Unfortunately, that description precludes most secular fiction.

270

Sounds like I'm preaching against music, TV, movies and books, oh – and beer and wine – doesn't it? I'm not though. If God hasn't revealed to us that reading such and such book or watching such and such movie is a sin – that's between us and God. I'm not willing to call any of those things vices – not even beer and wine. If we're talking about any sin at all here, it's the sin of omission of us not living up to our potential because we we're too busy entertaining ourselves. In that case, we could add Facebook, sports, shopping and time-consuming hobbies of all kinds as possible stumbling blocks.

> Basically everything on network television in the 9 p.m. prime-time spot is garbage, but even the lighter shows earlier in the evening are riddled with cultural messages that run contrary to the holy life we need to live to be mighty women of God.

God wants us to rest (Deut. 5: 12-15) and Jesus came that we might have abundant life. However, I don't think God ever intended those scriptures to be lived out as three hours of prime-time television after a hard day of work. There are plenty of restful and entertaining things we can do that edify us – one on the top of my list is spending quality time with family and friends. Other things, like gardening, walking, playing with a pet and enjoying nature, truly relax us without filling our mind with garbage. These things are so worthwhile.

I would like to challenge you to make the vast majority of your time today and every day move you toward your fullest potential as a mighty woman of God. That's the test: "Does this activity in which I'm engaged edify me? Does it make me a better person? Does it move me toward my fullest potential?" And then if it does, maybe we need to ask, "How much of this activity is enough?" Sleep, for instance, passes the test if we're talking about eight hours a night. At 10 or more hours a night, sleep ceases to move us to our fullest potential and starts to drag us down. Let women who don't have a God-given desire to be their best sleep 12 hours a night. You, the young woman who has persevered to the end of this book, you have much more important things to do with your life.

271

Wake up. Activate. Engage. Grow.

Hold this thought: I want to make the most of each day.

As Essential as Underwear

Stop listening to instruction, my daughter, and you will stray from the words of knowledge.

Proverbs 19:27

272

When I was in Salamanca, Spain, during my junior year of college, I made a lot of friends. And this is the tale of two of them. Charlotte is from The Netherlands. She and I had most of our classes together; we traveled together some and, in general, just hung out together a lot. Then there was Domingo; he is Spanish. He signed up for an exchange with an English-speaking student and we were assigned to each other. We met about once a week to have coffee and exchanged language knowledge. We started out in cafes, but progressed to doing a lot of fun things during our once a week exchange.

When my time in Salamanca drew to a close, I was sad to leave all my friends and as people often do, we exchanged addresses (that was before the era of e-mail). In one of my last meetings with Domingo, as we contemplated the distance that was about to be between us and how we would miss our weekly meetings, we made a pact with each other. We vowed to write to each other at least one time a year for the rest of our lives. One letter a year, doesn't seem too hard – but for the rest of our lives? It was truly the biggest commitment I had ever made.

I didn't make any such vow with Charlotte but I had every intention of keeping in touch with her anyway. And I did. Charlotte and I corresponded often, whereas I wrote only one letter a year to Domingo. I thought about Domingo more frequently than once a year, but only acted on those thoughts once a year.

My frequent correspondence with Charlotte led to me visiting her home. We traveled together to France, making a lot of memories, including losing each other in The Louvre – which is only funny in retrospect. I didn't make it to Spain on that trip, and on my next trip to Spain, I didn't come close to Salamanca to visit Domingo. However, I kept my vow and continued to write him at least once a year.

Charlotte and I continued a strong correspondence for many years, but a pattern was emerging. More and more time was lapsing between letters. First a couple of months, then six months, then just a Christmas card – and that for many years – until finally one year, I said to myself, "I doubt I'll ever see her again," and I quit sending the Christmas card. Now some five years have gone by and I count her among my memories.

The tale of Domingo hasn't ended yet. Domingo and I continue to write each other at least once a year. He sent pictures of his first born, Pablo, and his daughter, Eva, and we even e-mail now. With that slow, but steady commitment, we have maintained a relationship that's in its 20th year.

I finally did get back to Salamanca and my family and I stayed with Domingo and his wife, Maria Angeles. Our children became fast friends – and maybe even got a little crush on each other. As sure as I sit here today, I feel very confident that I will maintain a relationship with Domingo and his family for the rest of our lives. We have both proven ourselves faithful to the commitment we made.

Domingo and I are no more compatible than Charlotte and I were, the fundamental difference I see in the two scenarios is that I made a commitment to Domingo to keep in touch at a specific interval. It is the consistency of contact that made the difference. And that's what our verse is about – consistency of contact, not with a person, but with wisdom and instruction.

Just like relationships with people, your relationship to wisdom and knowledge must be maintained with consistency to remain alive and well and, to the contrary, if we neglect contact, we lose the relationship, however strong it may have started out.

There are some things that once we learn them, we can go long stretches without revisiting the information and yet it sticks with us. They say riding a bike is like that and I've found it to be true. There have been a couple of five-year stretches that I've gone without riding a bike. And when I have gotten back in the saddle after those long stretches, I immediately know how to work the machine!

Wisdom and knowledge are not like that. I made the mistake of thinking they were, but I found out first-hand that they are not. I used to read the Proverbs when I was a teenager. I was a wise teenager. I stayed out of trouble and avoided foolishness and stupid mistakes, not at all coincidentally, during the entire time I read the Proverbs – a period of several key years.

Then I stopped. Life got in the way. College totally disrupted my former routine and instead of reading Proverbs before I fell asleep, I was studying biology, partying, late-night chatting with friends. There was a residual effect of all that wisdom I had soaked in during my teen years, but when it finally wore off, do you know what was left? A fool. Turns out the only thing keeping me out of trouble all those years was my daily connection with the Wisdom of the Ages. Though being a fool again seemed like fun at the time, I don't have much to brag about now. I would be embarrassed to admit to many of my antics and I wouldn't want my daughter to know about them, for sure! I may have turned from those memories, but they have not disappeared. I left a trail of witnesses so thick I could never run for public office!

I am convinced that had I continued to attend church, talk to God and read the Proverbs with consistency, I would have had a very different youth – one much more suitable for a role model. I'm more like one of those reformed junkies who warns kids to stay away from drugs. I never did drugs; my folly was of the variety I am writing against in these pages – false intimacy, foolish spending, bad decisions.

Truly, if I could do one thing differently in my life, I would go back to the last day I thought about reading the Proverbs before I quit altogether, and instead of letting the thought pass, I'd pick up the good book and renew my commitment to consistent contact with wisdom and knowledge straight from the Creator of the Universe.

Be deliberate about your relationship with God. Make a commitment to stay in contact at least once a day. Begin to think about chatting with God as being as essential as changing your underwear each day. Can't you whisper a prayer while you're munching your lunch, brushing your teeth or taking a shower? (I don't recommend praying while you go to the bathroom though. I believe God deserves and wants more reverence than that.) If you will just start with a small commitment – like Domingo and I did – God will meet you there and your relationship will grow, just like mine and Domingo's relationship has. You'll find yourself voluntarily upping your rate of contact and spending more time thinking about pleasing God and more time in conversation with Him.

Hold this thought: I will tap into the source of all knowledge at least for a few minutes each day.

Tell Me if You Know!

I have not learned wisdom, nor have I knowledge of the Holy One. Who has gone up to heaven and come down? Who has gathered up the wind in the hollow of his hands? Who has wrapped up the waters in his cloak? Who has established all the ends of the earth? What is his name, and the name of his son? Tell me if you know!

Proverbs 30:3-4

276

So we're almost at the end of the Proverbs. We've prayed for understanding; we've meditated on the words; we've learned a thing or two. We're starting to feel equipped to take on life and come out on top. Then comes this royal dressing down. Who do we think we are? We haven't learned wisdom, we have no knowledge of God other than what God wants us to know about Him. We can't explain how God has done any of the above-listed accomplishments, not to mention those listed in the last few chapters of Job. After all this, have we even left "start"?

Going to Spain for my junior year abroad was the first time I had ever traveled out of North America. On the map, Spain looked so small, like if I just had a few good weeks, I could explore it sufficiently by train. Over weekends and holidays during an eight-month period, I ventured from my home base in Salamanca to the Spanish cities of La Coruña, Valladolid, Toledo, Madrid, Seville, Granada, Alicante, Avila, Barcelona and to many other smaller towns and a few places in Portugal. With each trip, it seemed I learned of a new place I would like to visit, such that by the time I left Spain, the list of places I still wanted to see was larger than the list of places I had been able to see. I still wanted to visit Santander, Bilbao, San Sebastian, Pamplona, Zaragoza, Segovia, Valencia, Malaga and Cordoba, to name the big ones.

When I finally got off my little dot on the map and started to explore other dots, I got an inkling of how big this earth is, how much it has to offer and how very much I can learn from it. I've been back to Europe a few times and each time I leave with this feeling of desperation – so many places to see, so little time. Then it hits me that I still have not been to Washington, Oregon, Idaho, Montana or Alaska – in my own back yard, compared to Europe.

This study of Proverbs that is now drawing to a close has been nowhere near exhaustive. It's a lot like my eight months in Spain. We've looked at a select few of the many places to visit in the Proverbs. And even if it were possible to thoroughly take in the wonders of the Proverbs during our lifetime, exploring the Psalms in the same manner we've contemplated each verse in this book would certainly take the rest of our lives.

Just like traveling on planet Earth, as soon as we get our first real taste of exploring God's wisdom, we realize we could pursue it with abandon for the rest of our lives and still have only scratched the surface. The most "well traveled" in God's word have long lists of places they still want to visit. We are just tourists where wisdom is concerned. We have not learned wisdom – we're not natives. For all our efforts, we can only know of God what God reveals to us, which in the grand scheme of things is not very much.

I congratulate you on getting this far in this book and putting forth the effort to apply God's wisdom to your everyday life, but don't stop here! Unlike Planet Earth with a finite number of destinations, there are no ends of the earth in God's world. You don't need a passport, money or a few dedicated weeks to make the trip. Set your itchy feet on the straight and narrow path and your journey has begun. Bon voyage.

Something to Shoot For

Here's the passage in Proverbs on which you may have thought this entire book would be based. I hope by now you know that there is so much more great advice for women in Proverbs, than just chapter 31. In fact, my experience in preparing this book has been that each time I would go through a chapter, let some time pass, then go through the same chapter again, I would identify different verses that would be good to include, and even on the same verses, different applications.

Proverbs is rich – as indeed the entire Bible is – but really, gals, Proverbs is rich! You can read it once a month for the rest of your life and never get all there is to get out of the Proverbs. In part, this is because each year life is changing and you'll relate better to some things in one season of life and better to others in another. My pass and review of Proverbs for your benefit has been specifically to glean applications for young, single women who need encouragement and wisdom to stay on the right track, or switch over to it. Later, if you marry and have children and have many more financial responsibilities than you do today, verses will pop out at you in such a way that it will seem you never read them before.

Remember this above all, to get wise and stay that way, you have to stay connected to the Scriptures – cultivate a relationship with the Word of God and don't neglect it. God will do the rest.

Now I will leave you with the infamous passage about the good woman. Might I suggest that you view this "laundry list" of positive traits as something to shoot for in life? I get worn out just reading through this and when I dare to tally the hours in this woman's day, they don't seem to add up, especially when I consider that she had no local grocer to butcher and trim her meat, no dairy to milk her goats and no Singer to sew her clothes. This gal is doing it all by hand! It's quite apt that the passage begins by saying, "Who can find such a wife?" Hey, but do note that she has servant girls – that's gotta help.

Here she is, our ideal, and you might be surprised at some of her characteristics. Again, like our Lady Wisdom, this wife is no pregnant, barefoot, illiterate, hush-mouthed helpmate, the likes of which Christendom has touted for centuries. She's full of surprises. Below, next to the New International Version of Proverbs 31:10-29, is my modern-day rendition to help you appreciate this woman more fully. And with this, I bid you farewell, fair maiden, with my sincere desire for your salvation and abundant life lived wisely.

A wife of noble character who can find? She is worth far more than rubies.	A high-quality wife can't be found on a reality show. Donald Trump, eat your heart out!
Her husband has full confidence in her and lacks nothing of value.	The man married to this woman could lose it all in an earthquake or tornado, and with his wife by his side, still feel like the luckiest man in the world.
She brings him good, not harm, all the days of her life.	She's like a lucky charm. It seems everything goes right because of her.
She selects wool and flax and works with eager hands.	She uses the best quality materials to stock her household – not excessive amounts of stuff – but what she has is the best.

280

She is like the merchant ships, bringing her food from afar.	She knows just where to get the best foods and cool, exotic stuff too. This gal doesn't feed her family on Hamburger Helper!
She gets up while it is still dark; she provides food for her family and portions for her servant girls.	She gets up at about 6 a.m. First thing on the agenda, feed the family and the hired help.
She considers a field and buys it; out of her earnings she plants a vineyard.	She's got a good head for business. She dabbles in real estate or the stock market and her investments net profit sufficient to expand her holdings.
She sets about her work vigorously; her arms are strong for her tasks.	Full of energy, she's not complaining about carpel tunnel or an aching back. Her energy begets more energy and people wonder, "How does she do it?"
She sees that her trading is profitable, and her lamp does not go out at night. In her hand she holds the distaff and grasps the spindle with her fingers.	She keeps good tabs on her finances and makes sure she remains in the black. She doesn't work by the clock either. She stays at the task until the job is done. When quitting time comes, she becomes productive at home – no prime-time boob tube for this gal.

She opens her arms to the poor and extends her hands to the needy.	She's a giver and never holds it over anyone's head. She always has room for one more plate at the table and can't resist slipping a dollar to the homeless guy at the stoplight.
When it snows, she has no fear for her household; for all of them are clothed in scarlet.	Her household never runs out of toilet paper! Her kids can always find socks that match. She knows the needs of her house and anticipates them so no one is ever without milk for their cereal.
She makes coverings for her bed; she is clothed in fine linen and purple.	She's a creative sort, handy with a needle and thread and it shows throughout her house. She's also got a great sense of style and doesn't leave home looking frumpy. Instead, she's dressed to turn heads.
Her husband is respected at the city gate, where he takes his seat among the elders of the land.	What's that old saying? Behind every good man is a great woman. And she certainly bears that out. Her husband is so confident in her love that he really believes he can do anything!

On my own now

She makes linen garments and sells them, and supplies the merchants with sashes.	This woman is a genius! She's a big business success and her secret was to find a need and fill it.
She is clothed with strength and dignity; she can laugh at the days to come.	Do you think she's worried that her hair is graying or face is wrinkling? This woman knows her inner beauty and strength will always make her outshine some spineless upstart.
She speaks with wisdom, and faithful instruction is on her tongue.	It's true, she's not much for idle chit-chat, but if you ever need some good advice, she's the one to go to.
She watches over the affairs of her household and does not eat the bread of idleness.	She's not relying on her husband to take care of things. She is fully engaged in her family's affairs. When she has some spare time, she reads a book, prays or does something else to build herself up.
Her children arise and call her blessed; her husband also, and he praises her: "Many women do noble things but you surpass them all."	Her kids appreciate her and secretly want to be like her (ha!). Her husband never complains about her to his coworkers. They envy his relationship. To her he says, "Oprah's got nothin' on you, Babe!"

Um, still here. I can't bear to say "Good-bye!" Please visit me on the Web at www.OnMyOwnNow.com and sign up for our free monthly e-zine *Single! Young Christian Woman*, available via e-mail or podcast. Each issue has more great tips on successful and wise living on your own. Also, visit the "Tool Box" link at www.OnMyOwnNow.com for loads of resources to assist in everything from small household repairs that can save you a ton of money, to finding something good to read, to preventing sport injuries – a little bit of everything you need to know on your own. And if you have a burning question about any aspect of independent living or anything we discussed in this book, I invite you to submit it to Dear Gabby, our chatty advice columnist.

283

Suggested Reading (or listening – some are available in audio as well)

There are tons of great books out there to help you continue the positive trajectory you are now on. I bet you're smart enough to find them on your own too. If you need a little help, go to www.amazon.com and find my book by searching the title or my name and then see what else Amazon suggests. Or, if that's not happening, here are a few of my favorites.

The Hiding Place by Corrie Ten Boom. If you need proof that God cares about the details and is still in the miracle-working business, this classic book is for you. Even if you don't need proof – read this book!

Lincoln the Unknown, also known as *The Unknown Lincoln* (they changed the title!) by Dale Carnegie. Did you think I was going to recommend a bunch of Stephen King novels? Get a history lesson with your dose of encouragement from this famous success story.

Simply Living: Modern Wisdom from the Ancient Book of Proverbs by Cecil Murphey. A lot like this book, but without the focus on young, Christian women, here's more good lessons from the Proverbs.

The 4:8 Principle by Tommy Newberry. Need more joy in your life? You've got what it takes; this book will help you discover it.

Overcoming an Enemy Called Average by John Mason. A modern book of proverbs in its own right. Pithy, but just right for reading while you wolf down breakfast or quick trips to the toilet.

Listening with My Heart by Heather Whitestone McCallum. If you need to ease into autobiography reading, here's the book for you. Reads quick and it's kind of neat to go behind the scenes of the whole Miss America thing (of which I am not a big fan).

Walking Man: A Modern Missions Experience in Latin America by Narciso Zamora. It's cool to watch God at work in the life of this humble Peruvian dude and his wife who have walked about 10,000 miles in their low-budget ministry.

The Good Earth by Pearl Buck. Well, it's my favorite book, how can I not suggest it!

And look for my upcoming book, *Purity's Big Payoff / Premarital Sex is a Big Ripoff,* an anthology of real stories that will validate your decision to wear white on your wedding day, available at www.OnMyOwnNow.com in 2010.

Bibliography

Lapsley, D., Aalsma, M. and Halpern-Felscher, B.L. (2005). *"In-vulnerability and risk behavior in early adolescence."* Society for Research in Child Development, Atlanta.
Read the full article at www.nd.edu, enter the article title in the search bar.

Groth, A. Nicholas, *Men Who Rape: The Psychology of the Offender*. Plenum Press, New York. 1981.

Poon, Chi-Sang and Young, Daniel L. "Nonassociative learning as gated neural integrator and differentiator in stimulus-response pathways." *Behavioral and Brain Functions* 2006, 2:29.
Read the full article (if you dare, not exactly light reading!) at www.behavioralandbrainfunctions.com/content/2/1/29.

Get Your Free Audiobook Download!

Listen on your MP3 player or your computer, or burn to CD and play in your car!

With the purchase of this book, you're entitled to one free download of the MP3 version of *On My Own Now: Straight Talk from the Proverbs for Young Christian Women who Want to Remain Pure, Debt-free and Regret-free* (abridged), read by the author, Donna Lee Schillinger.

Or…

If you've already read this to your heart's content and are wondering why in the world you would want to listen to it too, I'd like to thank you with another great audiobook: *Walking Man: A Modern Missions Experience in Latin America* by Narciso Zamora (abridged). Visit www.walkingman.ws for more information on this book.

To receive your free audiobook, log on to www.OnMyOwnNow. com and click on the "I Bought the Book" link. You'll be prompted to enter a password and it is:
Straight0Talk687349 (case sensitive). Then just follow the instructions – easy!

Donna Lee Schillinger's Top 5
Recommended Resources for Young Single Women

Angel Food If you're having trouble making ends meet, don't skimp on nutrition. Angel Food Ministries can provide good food for about one-third less than you could buy it in the store. Order and pick up once a month. Find a distribution point close to you at www.angelfoodministries.com or by calling 877-366-3646. Hundreds of thousands of people are saving a lot on groceries – why shouldn't you?

Center for Young Women's Health Just like that ping in your car that can end up being a $1200 repair, little body symptoms left untended can become major health issues. Don't go there. Before you visit the doctor and after too, log on to www.youngwomenshealth.org – a wealth of health info on the issues that affect young women.

Christian Social Networking Web Sites Whether its www.xianz.com, www.ChristianNation.com, www.FaithLight.com, www.HolyPal.com or another, Christian social networking is a much safer way to "hang out" on the Web.

ShapeFit This could be the best health and fitness Web site in the known universe. If you've got Internet at home, save the money you would spend on a gym, trainer or diet program and log on to www.shapefit.com and start exploring. My favorite feature is the Exercise Guides: Flash photographs of how to perform hundreds of exercises. www.shapefit.com

eHow.com Don't blow your stash on professional repairs to do a job you could handle yourself, if you only knew how. Here's the place to learn – and it's easy! www.ehow.com

Word on the Street Is...

"*On My Own Now* is an entertaining, smart and Biblically savvy friend for any girl to bring along when she leaves the nest."

Trish Perry
Author, *Sunset Beach* and *Too Good to Be True*

"Thoroughly readable and less 'lecture-ish' than similar books within the genre."

Kam Aures
RebeccasReads.com

"...Schillinger takes young women along a journey that will help them to make better, safer and more sound decisions."

Cheryl C. Malandrinos
The Book Connection blog

"...you can't go wrong with this as another resource to teach your young woman Biblical ideals and principles..."

Marta Hoelscher
The Cypress Times online

"Schillinger touches on all the major issues in a young woman's life – dating, money, friendship, work ethics, taking care of one's body and family. She does so in a very straight-forward, pull-no-punches manner and with a sense of humor."

Patrice Fagnant-MacArthur
www.spiritualwoman.net